T0372787

Official
Cambridge
Exam
Preparation

Kid's Box

New Generation

British English

Caroline Nixon &
Michael Tomlinson

CAMBRIDGE

Pupil's Book
with eBook

2

Language summary

Unit	Key vocabulary	Key language	Sounds and spelling
1 Hello again! page 4	**Character names:** Mr Star, Mrs Star, Stella, Simon, Suzy, Grandma Star, Grandpa Star, Marie, Maskman, Monty, Trevor **Numbers:** 1–10 **The alphabet** **Colours:** red, yellow, pink, green, orange, blue, purple, brown, black, white, grey	**Greetings:** Hello. We're the Star family. Who's he/she? This is my brother, Simon. He's seven, and this is my sister, Suzy. She's four. **Prepositions:** in, on, under	**Consonant sound:** *wh* (whale)
2 Back to school page 10	**School:** bookcase, board, cupboard, computer, desk, ruler, teacher, television, whiteboard **Character names:** Alex, Lenny, Meera **Numbers:** 11–20	How many (books) are there? There's / There isn't a (whiteboard). There are / aren't (11 desks). Is there (a ruler) on the (desk)? Yes, there is. / No, there isn't. Are there (19 pens) on the (desk)? Yes, there are. / No, there aren't.	**Long vowel sound:** *ee* (bee)
Marie's maths: What do we use in our maths class? page 16	**Trevor's values:** Be polite page 17		
3 Play time! page 18	**Toys:** alien, camera, board game, kite, lorry, robot, tablet, watch, teddy bear	this, that, these, those Whose is it / this (kite)? It's Stella's. Whose are these (shoes)? They're Sheila's.	**Long vowel sound:** *i–e* (kite)
4 At home page 24	**Furniture:** clock, lamp, mat, mirror, phone, sofa	mine / yours / his / hers Which shoes are (Simon's / Stella's)? The (grey) ones are (his/hers).	**Consonant sound:** *–se* (nose)
Marie's art: What can you do with origami? page 30	**Trevor's values:** Reuse and recycle page 31		
Review: units 1, 2, 3 and 4 page 32			
5 Meet my family page 34	**Family:** baby, cousin, mum, dad, grandma, grandpa **Character names:** Tony, Alice, Nick, Kim, Hugo, Lucy, May, Lenny, Sam, Frank	Lenny's hitting the ball. He isn't walking. What's Grandpa doing? **Verb + -ing spellings:** catching, cleaning, flying, getting, hitting, jumping, kicking, running, sitting, sleeping, talking, throwing	**Consonant sound:** *c*, *ck* and *k* (cat, clock, kitchen)
6 Dinner time page 40	**Food:** bread, chicken, chips, eggs, juice, milk, rice, water	Can I have some (bread), please? Here you are.	**Consonant sound:** *ch* (chicken)
Marie's science: Where does food come from? page 46	**Trevor's values:** Eat good food page 47		

1 Hello again!

1 🎧 2–3 Listen and point. Listen and repeat.

What's your name?
How old are you?

Stella

Mrs Star

Grandma Star

Mr Star

Simon

Grandpa Star

Suzy

2 Point and say.

Who's she?

She's Stella.

Vocabulary presentation 1: character names | **Language presentation 1:** greetings *Hello. Who's he/she?*

Listen and answer.

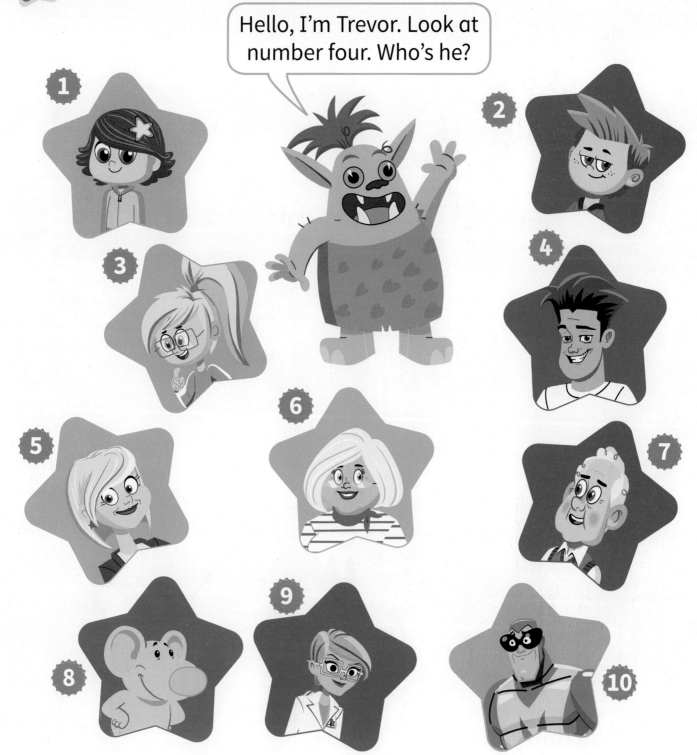

Hello, I'm Trevor. Look at number four. Who's he?

1 2 3 4 5 6 7 8 9 10

Ask and answer.

Look at number three. Who's she?

Stella.

1 5–6 Listen, point and repeat. Say the chant.

Aa
Bb
Cc
Dd
Ee
Ff
Gg
Hh
Ii
Jj
Kk
Ll
Mm
Nn
Oo
Pp
Qq
Rr
Ss
Tt
Uu
Vv
Ww
Xx
Yy
Zz

2 Play and say.

Hello. I'm grey. Which letters make my sound?

a, h, j, k

1

1

Ask and answer. Can you spell 'purple'? P-u-r-p-l-e.

2 **Put the colours in order. Write numbers.**

Black, blue, brown …

grey ☐ pink ☐ green ☐

orange ☐ brown ☐

white ☐ red ☐ blue ☐

purple ☐ yellow ☐

black 1

3

Spell and guess.

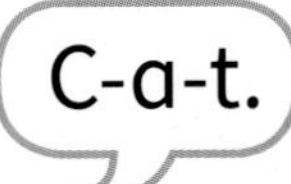
C-a-t.

Cat!

Monty's sounds and spelling

1
7

Watch and say.

Where's the white whale?
Next to the wheel!

2

Ask and answer.

Where's the white whale?

The white whale is on the wheel.

TOYS

Write it with me!

_ _ ale

1

1 8 Watch the video.

1
a, b, c, d, e, f, g …

2
Let's play a game. What's this colour? B-l-u-e.
I know. It's blue. My car's blue. Look!

3
Now, it's my turn. What's this word? F-o-u-r.
I know. That's four. Here are four pencils! My turn.

4
What's this, Trevor? P-u-r-p-l-e.
Er. Is it a pencil? Pencils are my favourite food.
No, Trevor. It's purple. Your hair's purple.

5
OK, Trevor. It's your turn.
Er. What's this? T-h-r-e-e.
Three. I've only got three pencils!

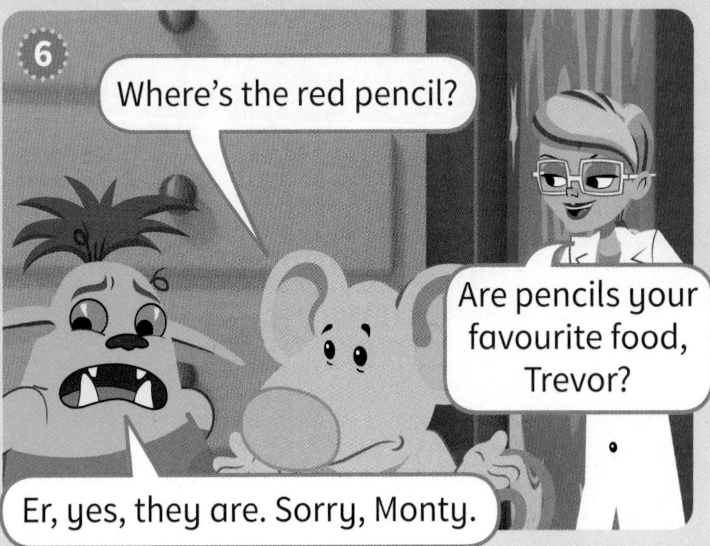
6
Where's the red pencil?
Are pencils your favourite food, Trevor?
Er, yes, they are. Sorry, Monty.

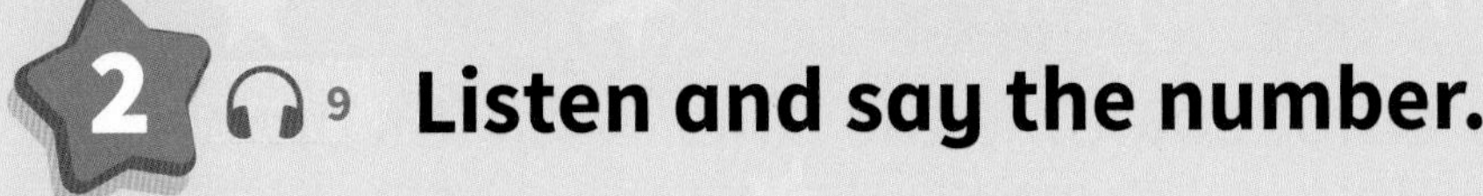

2 9 Listen and say the number.

2 Back to school

1 10–11 **Listen and point. Listen and repeat.**

board
teacher
cupboard
bookcase
ruler
desk

2 **Play and say.**

What colour is the ruler?

It's brown.

1 Listen and point. Say the chant.

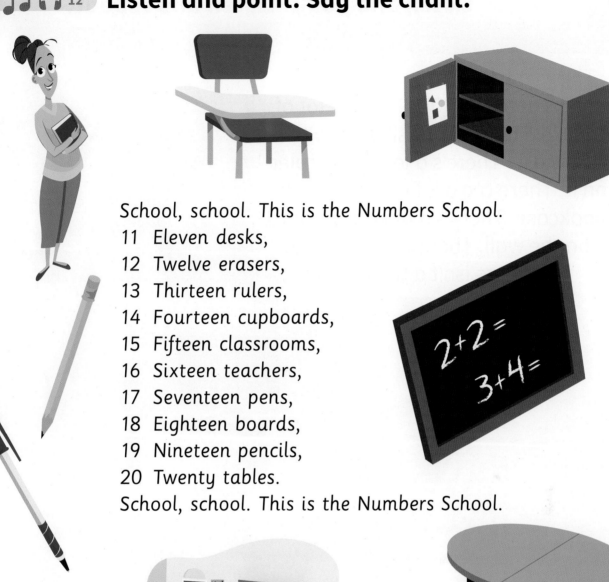

School, school. This is the Numbers School.
11 Eleven desks,
12 Twelve erasers,
13 Thirteen rulers,
14 Fourteen cupboards,
15 Fifteen classrooms,
16 Sixteen teachers,
17 Seventeen pens,
18 Eighteen boards,
19 Nineteen pencils,
20 Twenty tables.
School, school. This is the Numbers School.

2+2=
3+4=

2 Ask and answer.

How many desks are there?

Eleven.

1 13–14 Listen and point. Listen and repeat.

This is my classroom. How many desks are there? There are a lot of desks. That's my desk next to the bookcase. There's a long pink ruler on it. There are a lot of books in the bookcase. There's a big whiteboard on the wall. There's a computer, but there isn't a television.

2 Play and say.

There are nineteen chairs.

No.

15–16

Listen and sing. Do karaoke.

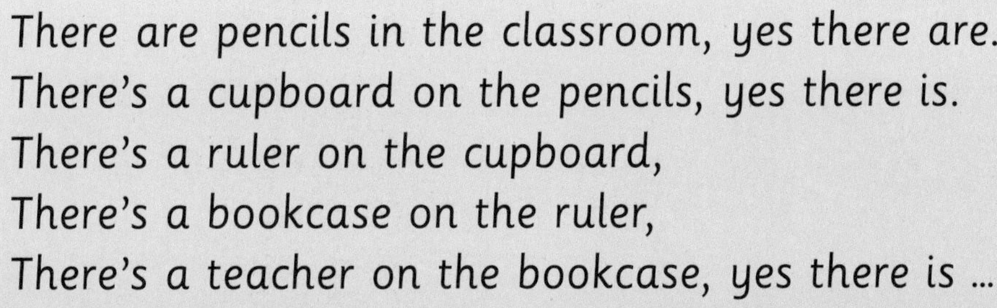

There are pencils in the classroom, yes there are.
There's a cupboard on the pencils, yes there is.
There's a ruler on the cupboard,
There's a bookcase on the ruler,
There's a teacher on the bookcase, yes there is …

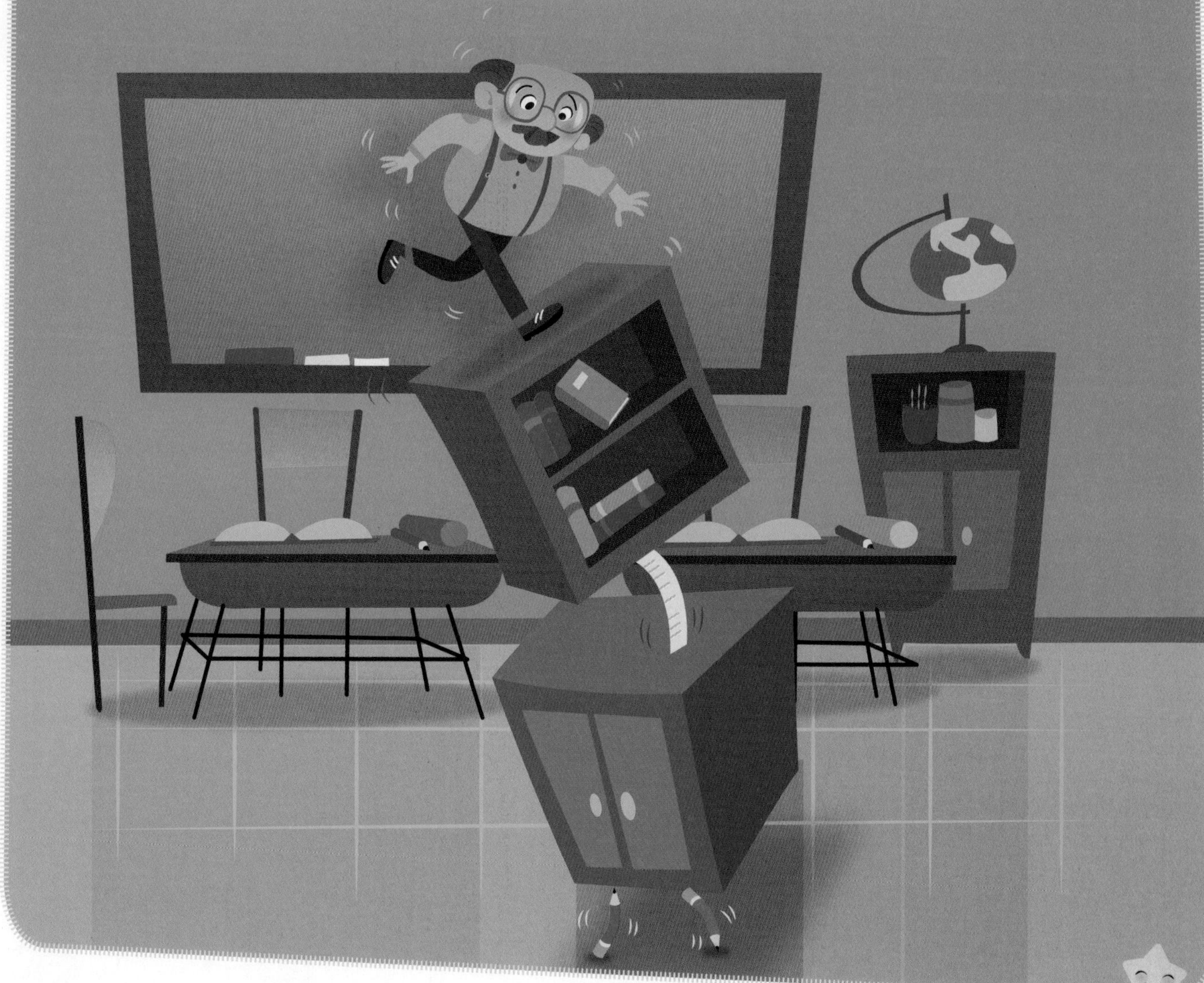

Ask and answer.

Where's the cupboard?

On the pencils.

Monty's sounds and spelling

1 17 Watch and say.

How many bees can you see?
Seventeen bees in the tree!

2 Ask and answer.

How many … are there?

There are …

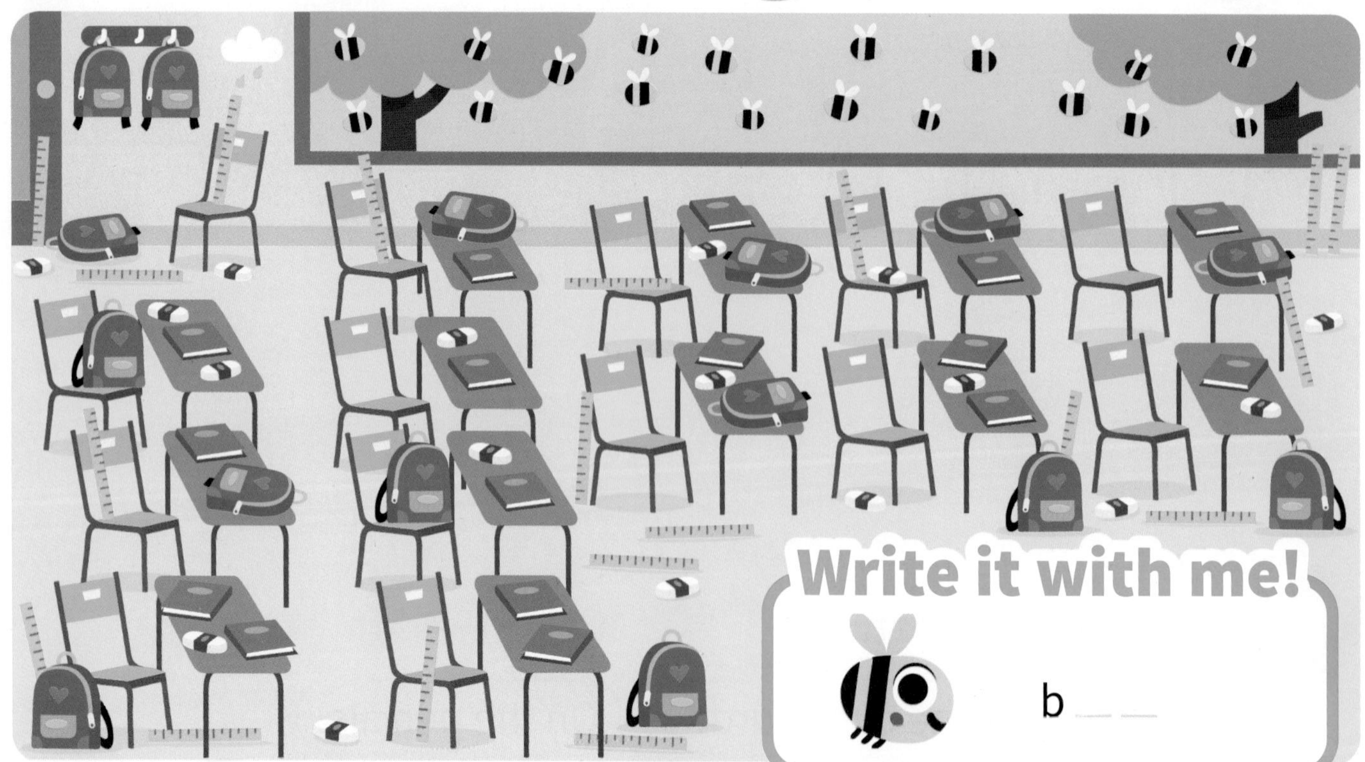

Write it with me!

b __ __

1 18 Watch the video.

1
OK, everybody. This bag is for school. Let's look.
MASKMAN
OK, Marie!

2
Hmm. Is there a ruler?
MASKMAN
Yes, there is. It's a 'Maskman' ruler.

3
Look, Marie. Here's an eraser.
Good! Can you put it in the bag, please, Monty?

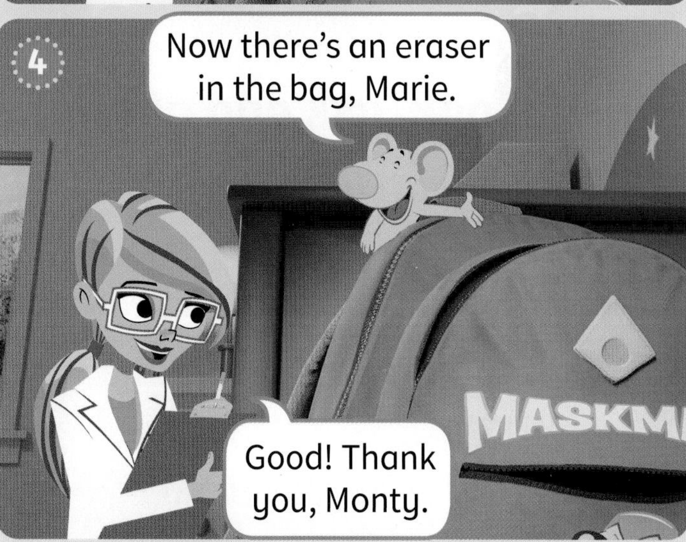
4
Now there's an eraser in the bag, Marie.
Good! Thank you, Monty.

5
Now, how many pencils are there?
There are 9, 10, 11 pencils.
12 COLOUR PENCILS

6
11 pencils! Where's the pencil? Trevor!
Sorry. Here you are. Pencils are my favourite food.
12 COLOUR PENCILS

2 19 Listen and say 'yes' or 'no'.

Marie's maths

What do we use in our maths class?

1 Watch and answer.

2 20 Listen and number.

a
b

c

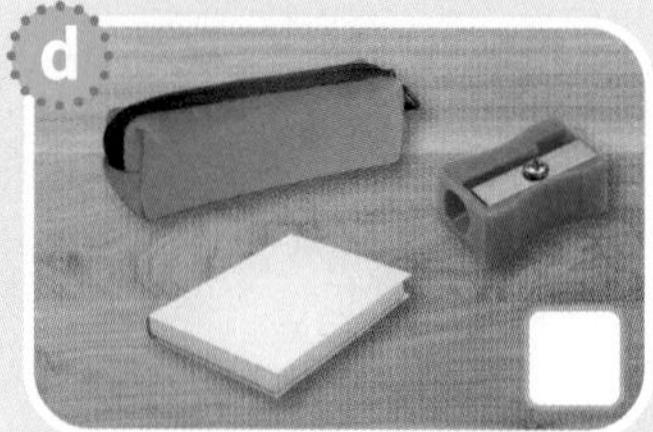

d

3 Look, ask and answer.

Is there a pen in Ben's pencil case?

Yes, there are four pens.

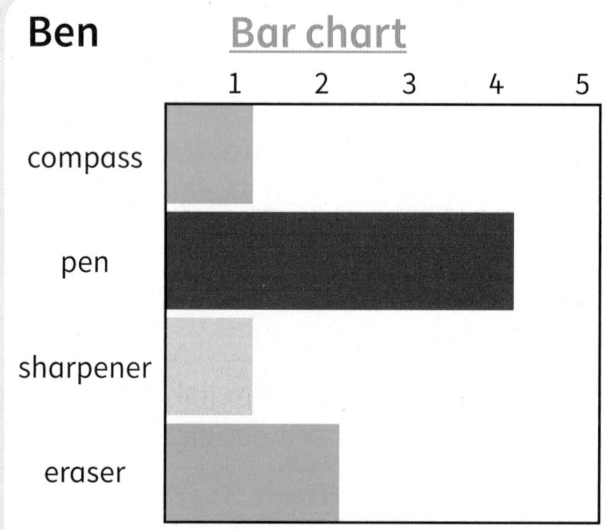

Ben
Bar chart
1 2 3 4 5
compass
pen
sharpener
eraser

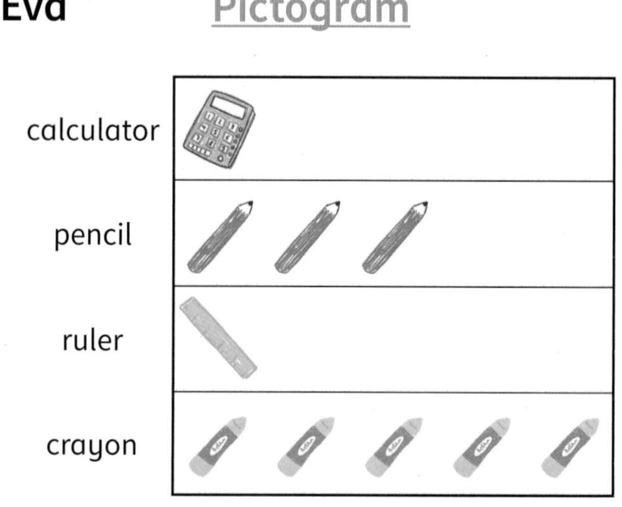

Eva
Pictogram
calculator
pencil
ruler
crayon

Fact

The first calculator is 190 years old. This is a part of it!

Project

Design a bar chart or pictogram.

Trevor's values

Be polite

1 21 **Listen and say the number.**

1

2

3

4

5

6

2 Act it out.

3 Play and say. Picture four! I can share my pencils.

3 Play time!

TOYS 4 U

1 22–23 **Listen and point. Listen and repeat.**

lorry

kite

Transport

Kites

Robots

Watches

watch

camera

Cameras

Board games

Teddy bears

alien

board game

robot

tablet

teddy bear

You Can Spell!

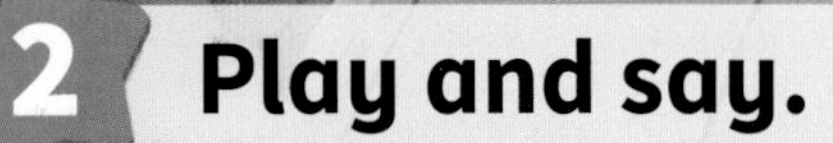

2 Play and say.

C-a-m-e-r-a!

That's camera!

3

1
24

Listen and say the number.

These are dolls. 19.

This is a robot. 17.

2
25

Listen and say 'yes' or 'no'.

1
26–27

Listen and point. Listen and repeat.

Why is the Sky Blue?
THINGS TH
ALL ABOUT BUN
HOW TO BUILD ROBOTS
HOW TO BUILD ROBOTS
Can you Spell?

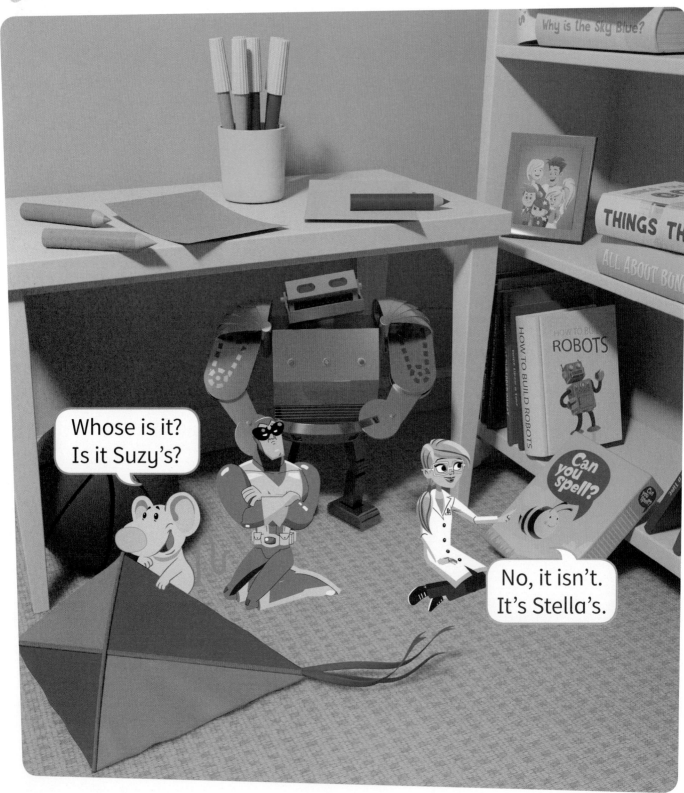

Whose is it?
Is it Suzy's?

No, it isn't.
It's Stella's.

2

Ask and answer.

Whose is this?

It's Suzy's.

Language practice 1: *this / these* | **Language presentation 2:** *Whose is it / this (kite)? It's Stella's.*

Listen and sing. Do karaoke.

SHEILA
TOM
JOHN
SUE

Whose is this jacket? ...
What? That black jacket?
Yes, this black jacket.
Whose is this jacket?
It's John's.
Oh!

Whose are these shoes? ...
What? Those blue shoes?
Yes, these blue shoes.
Whose are these shoes?
They're Sheila's.
Oh!

Whose is this skirt? ...
What? That purple skirt?
Yes, this purple skirt.
Whose is this skirt?
It's Sue's.
Oh!

Whose are these trousers? ...
What? Those brown trousers?
Yes, these brown trousers.
Whose are these trousers?
They're Tom's.
Oh!

Ask and answer.

Whose are these trousers?

They're Tom's.

Monty's sounds and spelling

1 30 **Watch and say.**

Hide the five kites and ride the white bike!

2 **Play and say.**

Which is my kite?

Is it the blue and red kite?

Write it with me!
k__t__

1 31 Watch the video.

1
Whose is this robot?
It's Simon's.

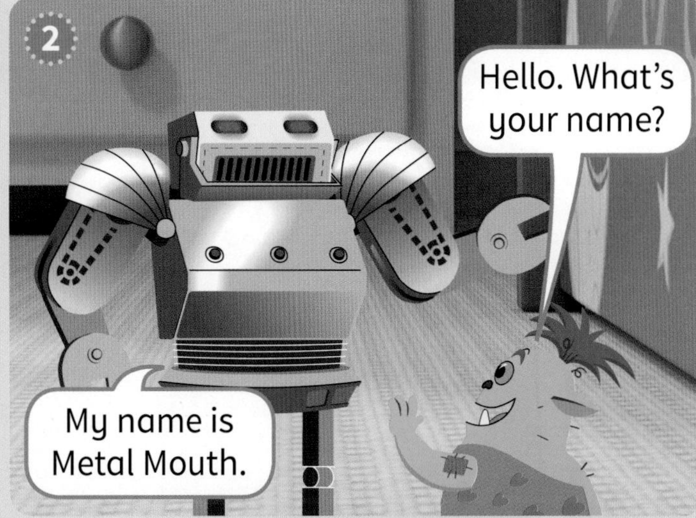
2
Hello. What's your name?
My name is Metal Mouth.

3
Oh. Can you walk, Metal Mouth?
I can walk and I can talk.

4
ugly
Well, I can walk. I can talk, and I can spell. U-g-l-y.

5
I know! I know! It's ugly!
Yes, it is … and it can't fly.

6
Maskman! Say 'sorry' please.
Sorry.
It's OK, Maskman. You're a superhero and you're Simon's favourite toy.

2 Act out the story.

4 At home

1 32–33 Listen and point. Listen and repeat.

mirror

mat

clock

sofa

phone

lamp

2 Ask and answer.

What colour's the clock in the kitchen?

It's orange.

1 34 Listen and point. Say the chant.

There's a mirror in the bathroom,
And a phone in the hall.
A sofa in the living room,
A clock on the wall.
There's a lamp on the table,
And a mat next to the bed.
There's a boat in the bath,
And the boat is red.

2 35 Listen and correct.

There's a girl sitting on the sofa.

There's a boy sitting on the sofa.

1
36–37
Listen and point. Listen and repeat.
Are those blue socks yours, Simon?
No, they aren't mine.
2
Ask and answer.
Is it mine or yours?
It's mine.

Language presentation and practice 1: possessive pronouns *It's mine. Are those yours?*

Listen and sing. Do karaoke.

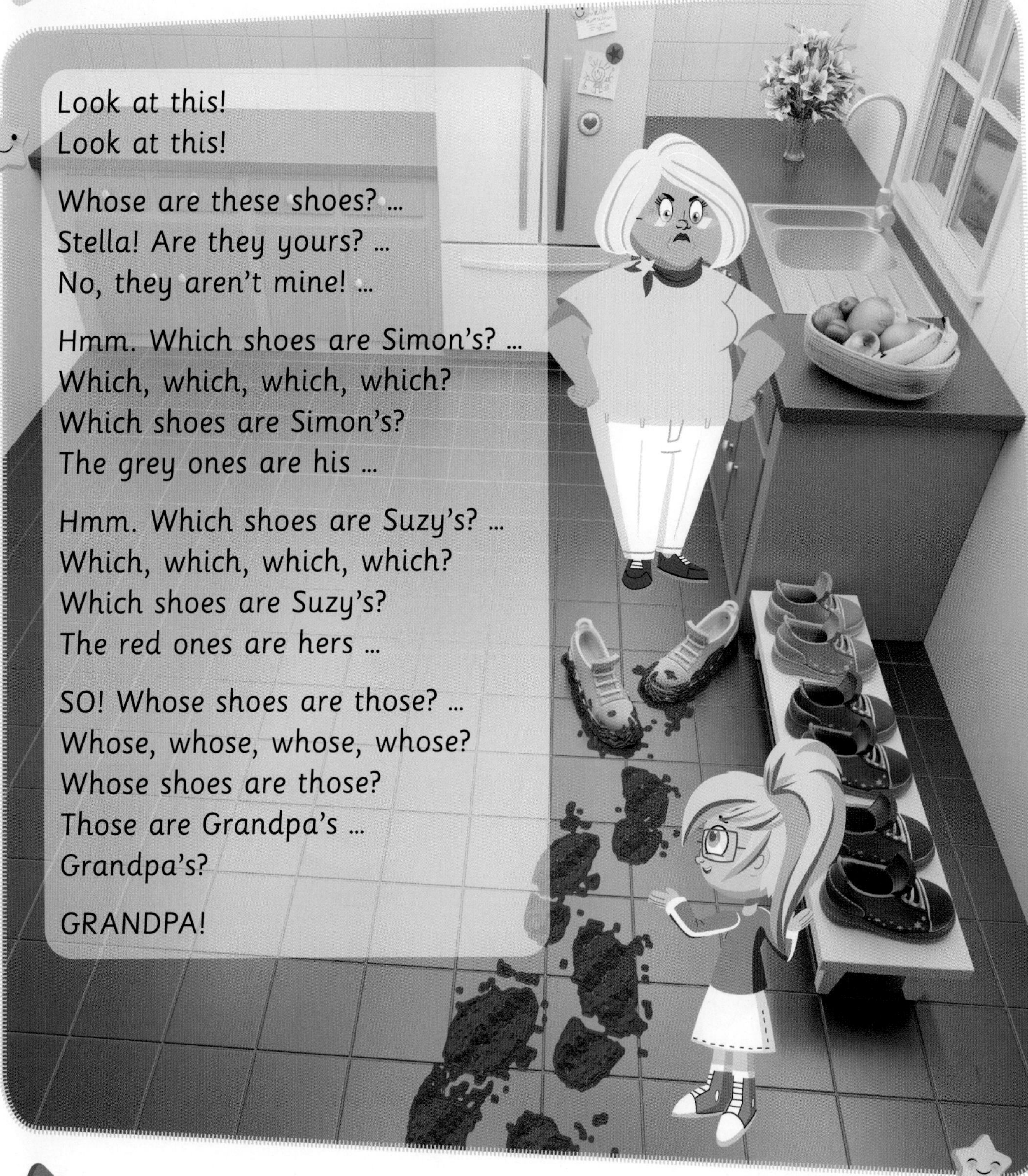

Look at this!
Look at this!

Whose are these shoes? ...
Stella! Are they yours? ...
No, they aren't mine! ...

Hmm. Which shoes are Simon's? ...
Which, which, which, which?
Which shoes are Simon's?
The grey ones are his ...

Hmm. Which shoes are Suzy's? ...
Which, which, which, which?
Which shoes are Suzy's?
The red ones are hers ...

SO! Whose shoes are those? ...
Whose, whose, whose, whose?
Whose shoes are those?
Those are Grandpa's ...
Grandpa's?

GRANDPA!

Ask and answer.

Which bag is yours?

The red one's mine.

Monty's sounds and spelling

1 40 **Watch and say.**

Whose are those noses? Look and choose!

2 **Ask and answer.**

Whose is this nose?

It's Simon's.

11 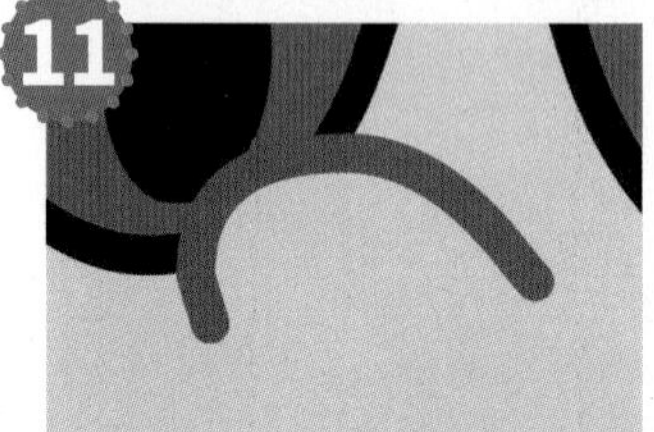

12 

13 

14 

15 

16 

17 

18 

Write it with me!

no __ __

4

1 41 Watch the video.

1
Let's play hide and seek.
Trevor, close your eyes and count to 20.

2
… 17, 18, 19, 20. I'm coming.

3
Where are they? Whose is that tail? Ha ha! I can see you, Monty. You're under the armchair.
OK. Well done, Trevor.

4
Look. Whose feet are those? Come out, Maskman. We can see you next to the bookcase.
CONSTRUCTION
THE SOLAR SYSTEM
MAKE YOUR OWN COSTUMES!
THE SOLAR SYSTEM
MAKE YOUR OWN COSTUMES!

5
Now, where's Marie?
Marie's in the cupboard. Look! That's her hair.

6
Eeeek! What's that?
I win!
It's a toy horse.

2 42 Listen and say the number.

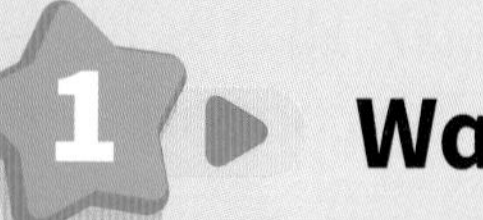
Marie's art

What can you do with origami?

1 ▶ **Watch and answer.**

2 **Match and say.**

Number 1. Star!

box ☐ bird ☐ heart ☐ star [1] flower ☐

1
2
3
4
5

3 🎧 43 **Listen and write.**

~~bird~~ box flower heart star

Clara	Chen	Flora	Tina	Adam

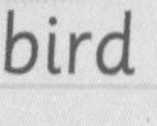 bird				

Fact

The world record for the number of origami elephants is 78,564!

Project

Make origami games.

Trevor's values

Reuse and recycle

44 **Listen and say the number.**

1

2

3

4

Ask and answer.

What's this?

It's an elephant.

What's it made from?

It's made from bottles.

What do you reuse at home?

I reuse … at home.

paper

bottles

plastic bags

Review Units 1, 2, 3 and 4

1 45 Listen and say the number.

11
12
13
14
15
16
17
18
19
20

2 Look and say.

In picture one there's a blue rug on the floor, but in picture two there's a purple rug on the floor.

1

2

Play the game. Ask and answer.

What number is this? 19.

What number is this?
16
What are these?
What room is this?
What colour is the sofa?
What number is this?
19
What's this?
Start

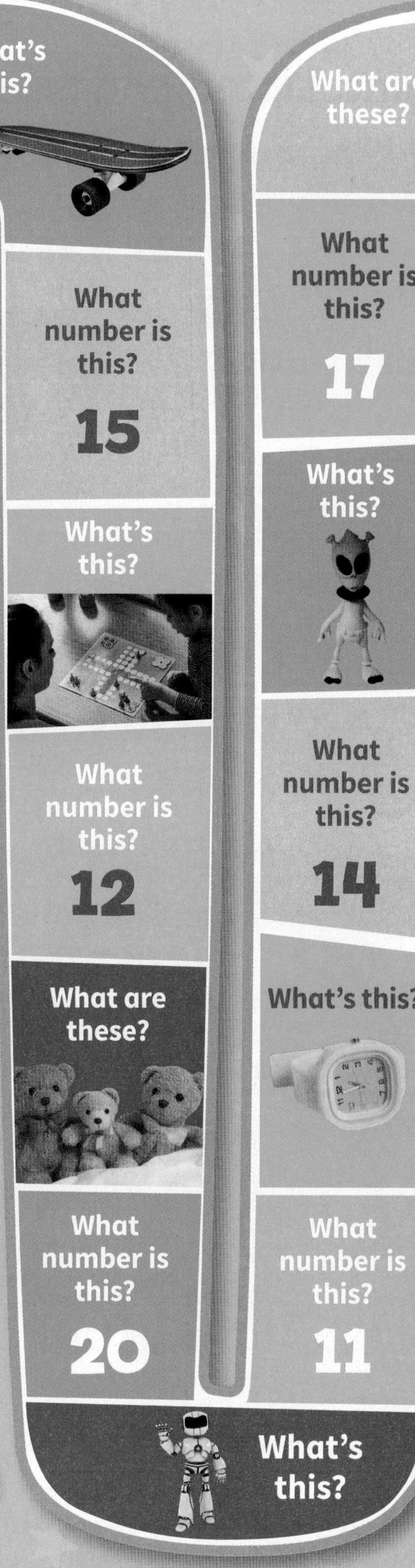

What's this?
What number is this?
15
What's this?
What number is this?
12
What are these?
What number is this?
20
What's this?
What are these?
What number is this?
17
What's this?
What number is this?
14
What's this?
What number is this?
11

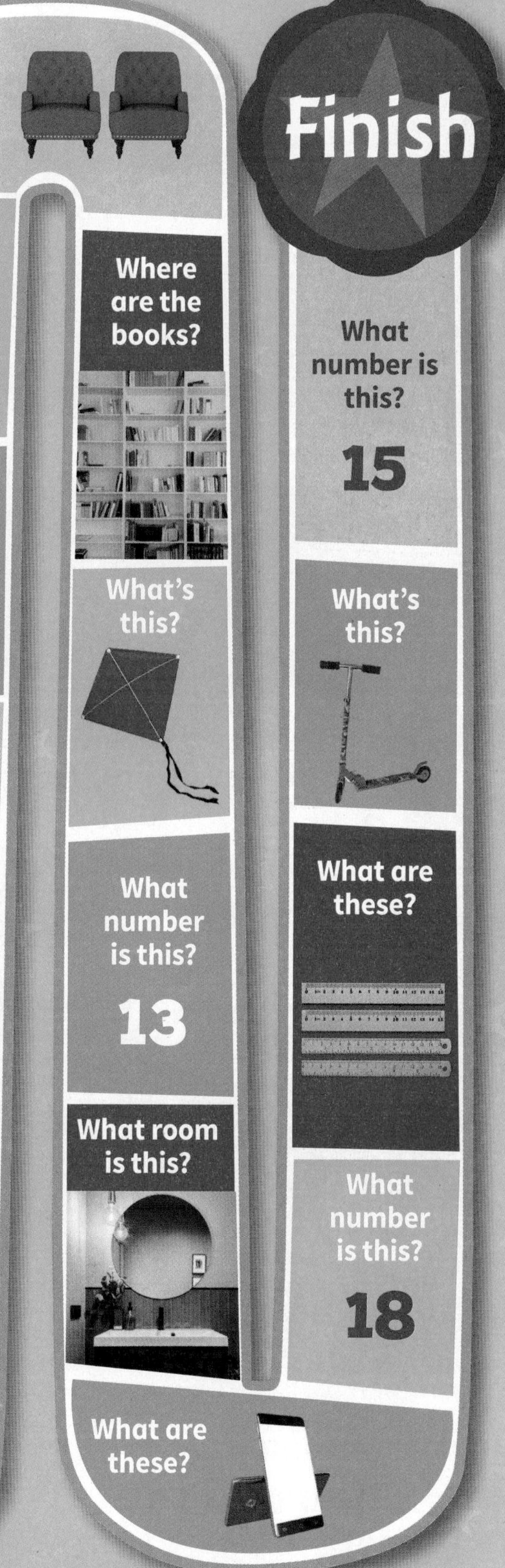

Finish
Where are the books?
What's this?
What number is this?
13
What room is this?
What are these?
What number is this?
15
What's this?
What are these?
What number is this?
18

5 Meet my family

1 46–47 Listen and point. Listen and repeat.

dad
mum
grandpa
cousin
baby
grandma

2 Play and say.

Spell 'baby', please.

B-a-b-y.

1
48

Listen and answer.

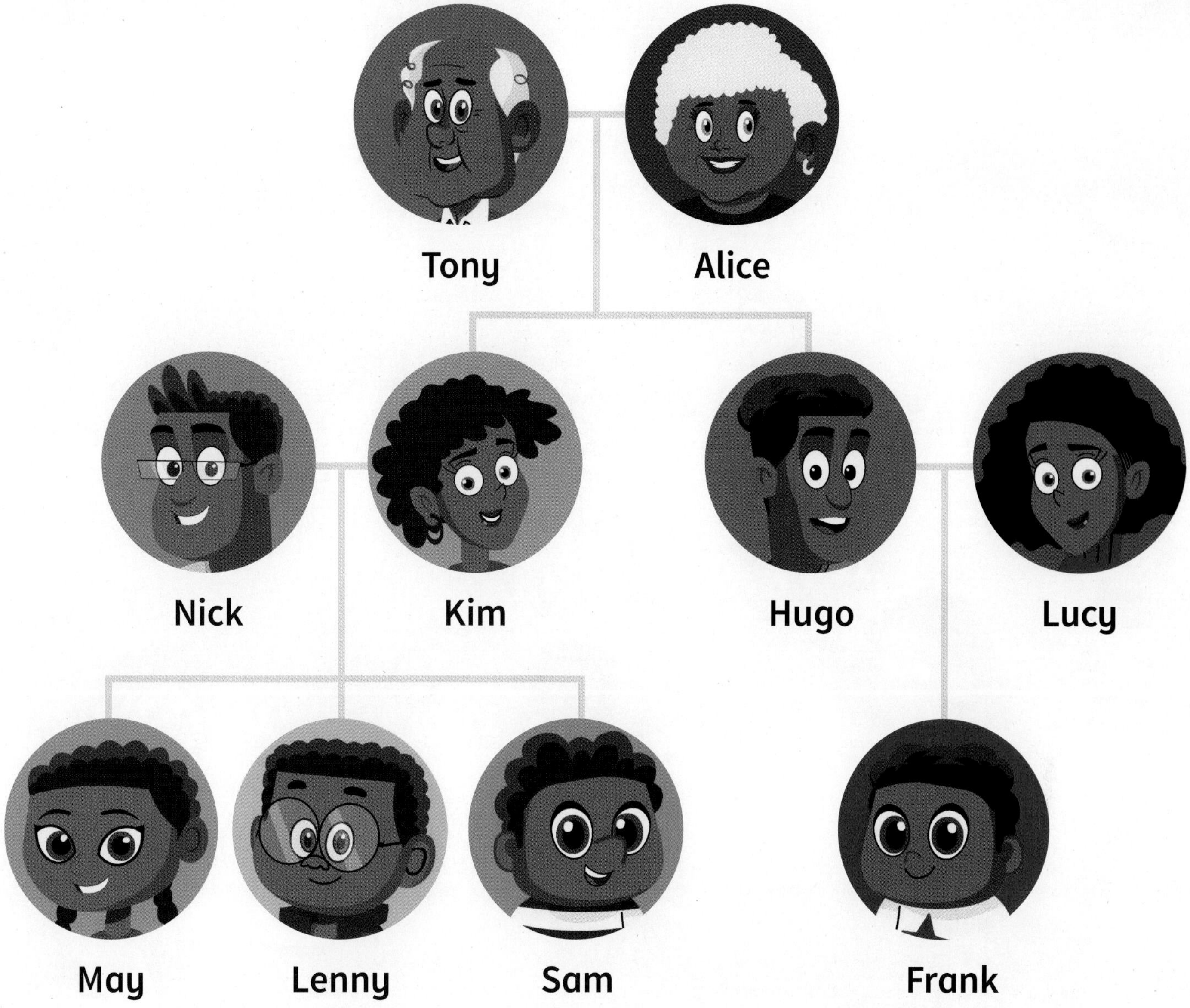

Tony Alice

Nick Kim Hugo Lucy

May Lenny Sam Frank

2

Look and say.

He's Lenny's father.

Nick.

3

Play and say 'yes' or 'no'.

Kim is Hugo's sister.

Yes.

1
49
Listen and say the number.
11
12
13
14
15
16
17
18
19
20

2 Make sentences. Use the words in the box.

The dog's getting the ball.

getting	throwing	catching	flying	talking	jumping
sitting	hitting	cleaning	running	kicking	sleeping

Language presentation and practice 1: present continuous *Lenny's hitting the ball.*

1 50–51 Listen and sing. Do karaoke.

My grandpa isn't walking,
He's flying my favourite kite.
My grandma's cleaning the table,
It's beautiful and white.
My father's playing baseball,
He can catch and he can hit.
My cousin's got the ball now,
And now he's throwing it.

My baby sister's sleeping,
She is very small.
My brother isn't jumping,
He's kicking his football.
Hey!

My grandpa isn't walking,
He's flying my favourite kite.
My grandma's cleaning the table,
It's beautiful and white.
My mother's sitting reading,
Her book is big and grey.
And me? I'm very happy,
I can run and play ...

2 Ask and answer.

What's Grandpa doing?

He's flying a kite.

Monty's sounds and spelling

1 Watch and say.

Look, crocodile! A cat in a coat is taking your cup!

2 Look and choose. Ask and answer.

What's the cat doing?

The cat's cleaning a clock.

cow | cat | snake | crocodile | duck | monkey

Write it with me!

A __at with a __up.

5

1 53 Watch the video.

1
Ooh! What's he doing to those shoes, Marie?
He's cleaning them, Trevor.

2
Hello, Trevor! Look at me! I'm driving Suzy's yellow lorry.

3
Hello, Maskman. What are you doing?
I'm flying my helicopter. I'm a superhero.

4
Hello, Marie. What are you doing?
I'm cleaning my shoes.

5
What are you doing, Trevor?
I'm cleaning the doll's house.

6
Oh no!

2 54 Listen and say the number.

6 Dinner time

1 55–56 **Listen and point. Listen and repeat.**

rice
milk
juice
water
bread
chips
eggs
chicken
RICE
MILK
SO FRESH OJ
Cake Mix

2 **Ask and answer.**

What can you see in the kitchen?

I can see bread.

6

1
57–58

Listen and sing. Do karaoke.

It's morning, it's morning.
We're having breakfast with our mum.
Bread and milk, bread and milk.
It's morning, it's morning.

It's lunchtime, it's lunchtime.
We're having lunch with our friends.
Egg and chips, egg and chips.
It's lunchtime, it's lunchtime.

It's afternoon, it's afternoon.
We're having tea in the garden.
Chocolate cake, chocolate cake.
We're having tea in the afternoon.

It's evening, it's evening.
We're having dinner with Mum and Dad.
Chicken and rice, chicken and rice.
It's evening, it's evening ...

2

Point, ask and answer.

What's this?

It's chocolate cake.

What are these?

They're chips.

1 59–60 Listen and answer. Listen and repeat.

Can I have some brown bread, please?
Here you are.
APPLE
SO FRESH OJ
Ingredients: Oranges.

2 Act it out.

Language presentation: polite requests *Can I have some bread, please? Here you are.*

6

1

Play bingo.

2

Read and answer.

Hello. My name's Alex. I'm Simon's friend. It's lunchtime and I'm having … and … for lunch. … isn't my favourite lunch. My favourite lunch is … . In the morning my favourite breakfast is … and …, and my favourite dinner is … and … .

1 What's his favourite breakfast?
2 What's his favourite lunch?
3 What's his favourite dinner?

Monty's sounds and spelling

1 61 **Watch and say.**

The chicken's lunch is cheese, chips and chocolate!

2 **Choose and draw. Ask and answer.**

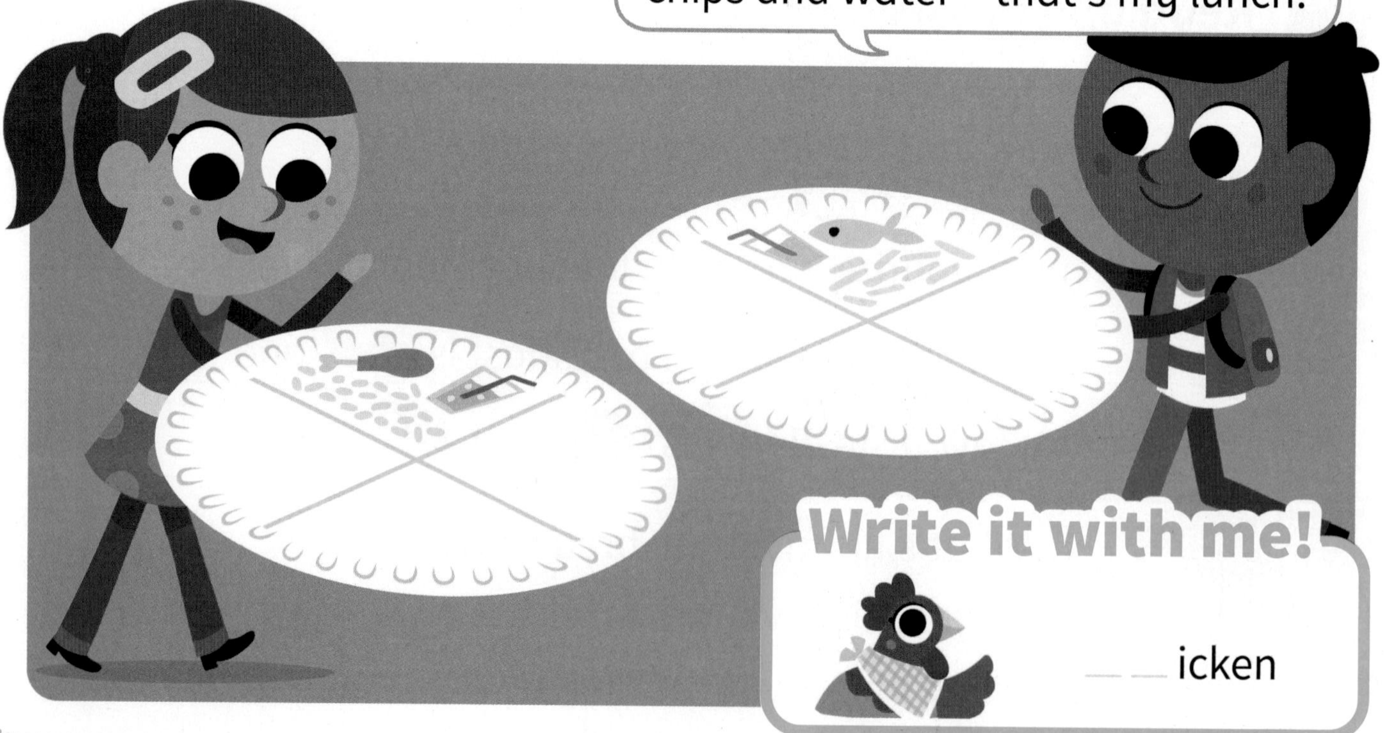
What's for lunch?
On my plate there's some fish and chips and water – that's my lunch!
Write it with me!
__ __ icken

62 Watch the video.

1
I'm having tomatoes and carrots.

2
Can I have some apple juice, please?

3
Here you are.
Is there any chocolate cake?

4
No, there isn't, but there's some chocolate ice cream.

5
Is this orange juice yours, Monty?
No, it isn't mine. It's Marie's.

6
What are you eating, Trevor? Is it chicken?
Er, no. It isn't chicken. It's a long brown pencil.
Oh, Trevor!

2 63 Listen and say 'yes' or 'no'.

Marie's science

Where does food come from?

1 ▶ **Watch and answer.**

2 **Look and say.**

Meat is from animals.

Carrots are from plants.

3 **Look, read and complete.**

vegetables cows meat milk plants yoghurt

My favourite food is ________ .
It comes from the ________ of
animals, like ________ and sheep.

Nick

Maya

My favourite food is ________ . They
come from ________ . My family is
vegetarian. We don't eat ________ .

There are lots of different ice cream flavours: cheese ice cream, potato ice cream and fish ice cream!

Fact

Project

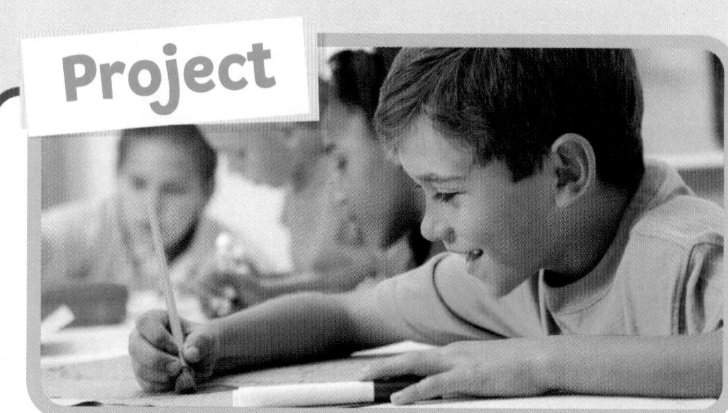

Design a food poster.

Trevor's values

Eat good food

1 64 **Listen and say the number.**

Breakfast

Lunch

Dinner

2 Ask and answer.

What's number one?

It's a bad breakfast.

What's number four?

It's a good lunch.

7 At the farm

1 65–66 **Listen and point. Listen and repeat.**

donkey
sheep
cow
spider
goat
duck
lizard
frog
Entrance

2 **Ask and answer.**

What's this?

It's a cow. Moo!

7

1
67–68

Listen and sing. Do karaoke.

Cows in the kitchen, moo moo moo,
Cows in the kitchen.
There are cows in the kitchen, moo moo moo,
What can we do, John Farmer?

Sheep in the bedroom, baa baa baa …

Ducks on the armchair, quack quack quack …

Frogs in the bathroom, croak croak croak …

Chickens in the cupboard, cluck cluck cluck …

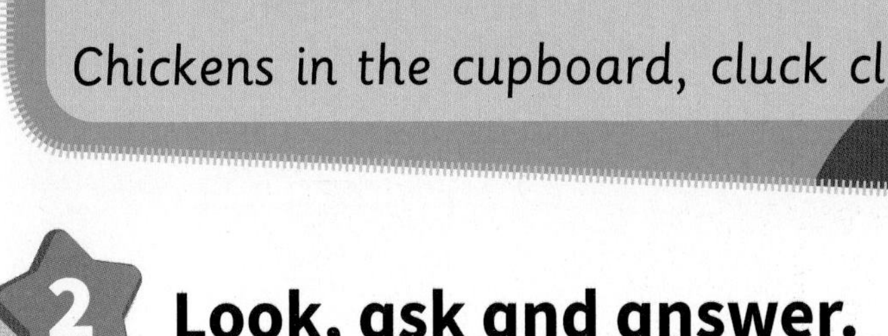

2 Look, ask and answer.

Where's the donkey?

It's in the garden.

1 69–70 Listen and answer. Listen and repeat.

Animal ABC's
THINGS THAT GO!
ROBOTS
So do I.
I love horses.
I don't.

2 Act it out.

Language presentation: agreeing and disagreeing *I love horses. So do I. I don't.*

1 Listen and point. Say the chant.

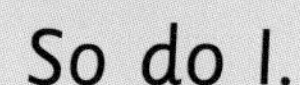

I love watermelon.	So do I.
I love pineapple.	So do I.
I love bananas.	So do I.
I love oranges.	So do I.
I love mangoes.	So do I.
I love coconuts.	So do I.
I love lemon and lime.	Hmm. So do I.
I love onions.	I don't. Goodbye.

2 Read and choose. Say and play.

I like cats.

So do I.

I like spiders.

I don't.

1 I like 

3 I like 

2 I love 

4 I love 

Monty's sounds and spelling

1 72 **Watch and say.**

A slow snail, a scary snake and a speedy spider!

2 **Play and say.**

They're brown and they've got long legs.

Spiders!

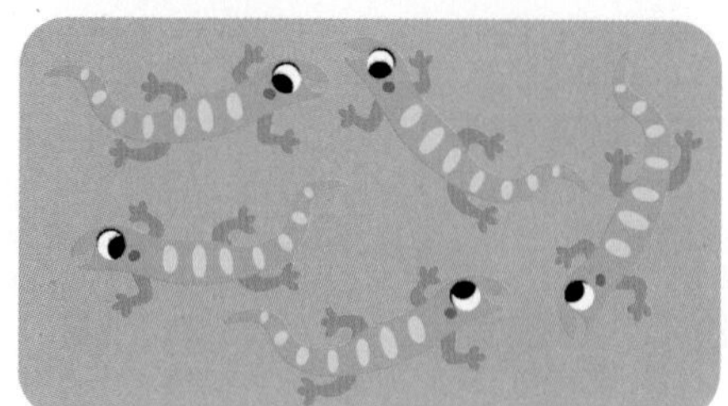

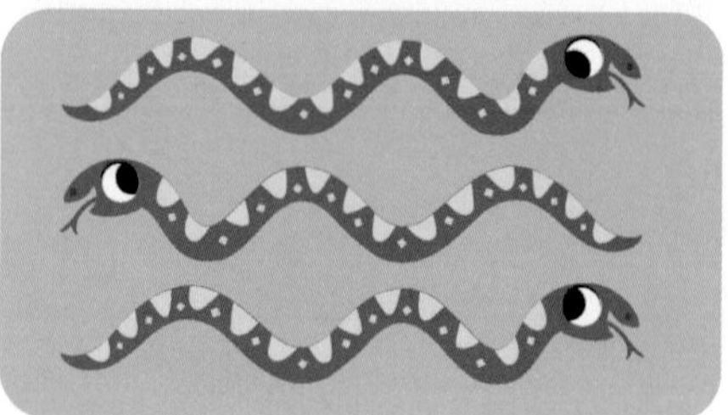

Write it with me!

A ___ ake and
a ___ ider!

1 73 Watch the video.

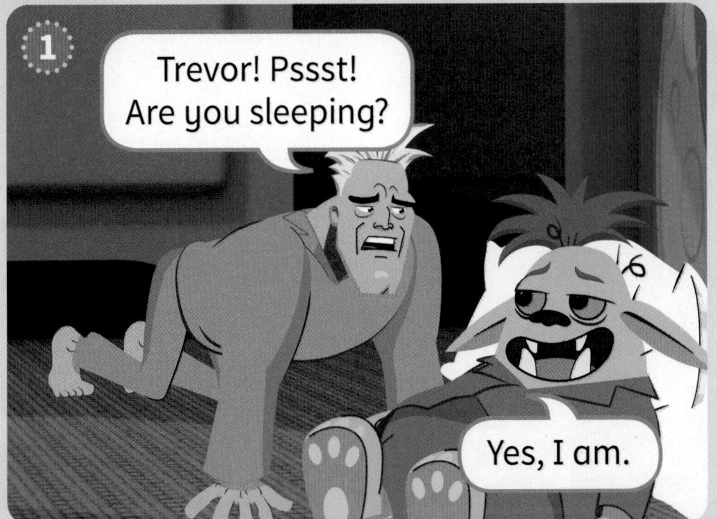
1
Trevor! Pssst!
Are you sleeping?
Yes, I am.

2
Trevor! Maskman!
Can you be quiet, please?
I'm trying to sleep!

3
I can't sleep.
Well, count sheep, Maskman.

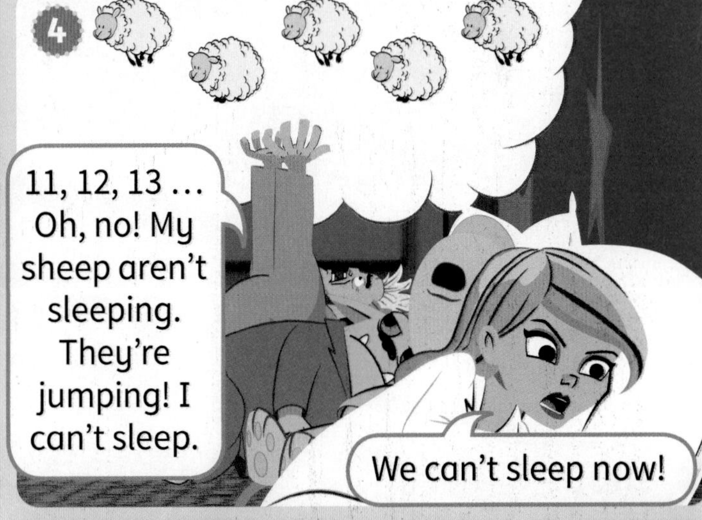
4
11, 12, 13 … Oh, no! My sheep aren't sleeping. They're jumping! I can't sleep.
We can't sleep now!

5
OK, let's talk about farms. Farm dogs can get sheep. Farm cats can catch mice. And we get milk from cows.
Yes … yes, I know. Maskman!

6
What are you doing, Maskman?
I'm sleeping, Marie. Goodnight.

2 Act out the story.

8 My town

1 74–75 Listen and point. Listen and repeat.

park

flat

hospital

shop

café

street

Pete's Pets

Flora's Flowers

Smart Clothes

PARK

TOYS 4 U

Good Food Café

Small Feet Shoes

Good Food Café

2 Ask and answer.

Spell 'café', please.

C-a-f-e.

1 Read and answer.

Shoes
TOM'S TOYS
FINN'S
FRUIT + VEG
Café

1 Where's the woman with the dog?
2 How many pineapples are there?
3 How many dogs are there?
4 Where's the boy with the kite?
5 What colour are the boots in the shoe shop?
6 Where are the lemons?
7 What colour's the bus?

2 Ask, count and answer.

How many skateboards are there?

There are two skateboards.

babies cars children coconuts lemons men
pineapples planes skateboards trains women

Lenny's mum's in front of me.
Who's in front of Grandma?
Simon.

1 76 Listen and point.

2 Ask and answer.

Language presentation: prepositions *behind, between, in front of*

8

1
77–78

Listen and sing. Do karaoke.

Put two books on the table ...
Put a pencil between the books ...
Put a pencil behind your head ...
Put a book in front of your nose ...
Put a book under your chair ...
Put a pencil behind your ear ...
Put two books on your head ...
Put them all back on the table,
And now, now, sit down.

2

Read and say. Write.

There's a black book next to the armchair. There's a brown book the dog and there's a purple book the yellow bag. There's an orange book the sofa and the table.

Monty's sounds and spelling

1 79 **Watch and say.**

They're playing in the park.
Hippo is hopping! Panda is jumping!

2 **Ask and answer.** Where's the panda? Next to the snake.

TOYS

Write it with me!

hi____o and
___anda

1 80 Watch the video.

1
Aaagh! Look behind you. It's behind you!
Ooooh! I can't look!

2
Oh, no. It's 'Dogzilla', the monster dog.

3
I'm coming, children.
Maskman's our superhero.

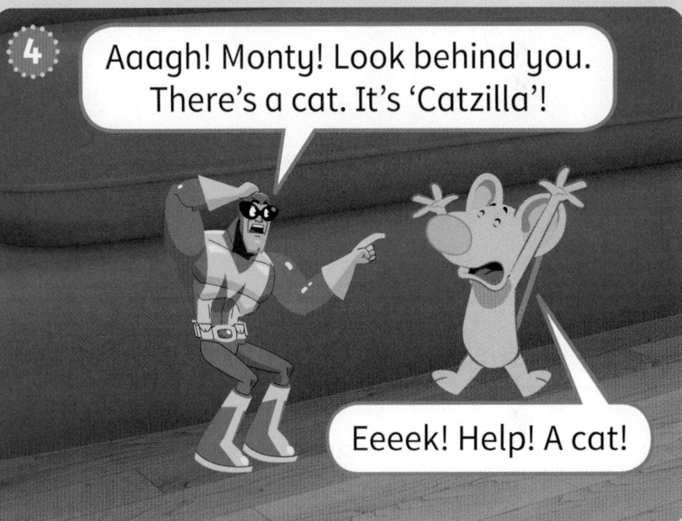
4
Aaagh! Monty! Look behind you. There's a cat. It's 'Catzilla'!
Eeeek! Help! A cat!

5
Ha ha ha.
It isn't funny!

6
Look! There's a dog. It's behind you.
Eeeek! Help! There's a dog. It's 'Dogzilla'! Help!

2 81 Listen and say the number.

Marie's geography

Where do we live?

1 Watch and answer.

2 Read and match. Write.

1. This is my town. It isn't very small and it isn't very big. It's got shops, a supermarket and a cinema. It's next to the sea.

2. This is my village. It's small! It's got two shops, a bakery and a little library.

3. This is my city! It's very big. It's busy with people, cars and buses every day.

a 

b 

c 

3 Find and write the words. Ask and answer.

bakery   cinema   library   playground   school

A
B
C
D
E
1
2
3
4

1 C1 = library
2 B3 =
3 C3 =
4 E2 =
5 A4 =

Fact

This is a floating village in Thailand. All the people live on boats!

Project

Make a town plan and fact file.

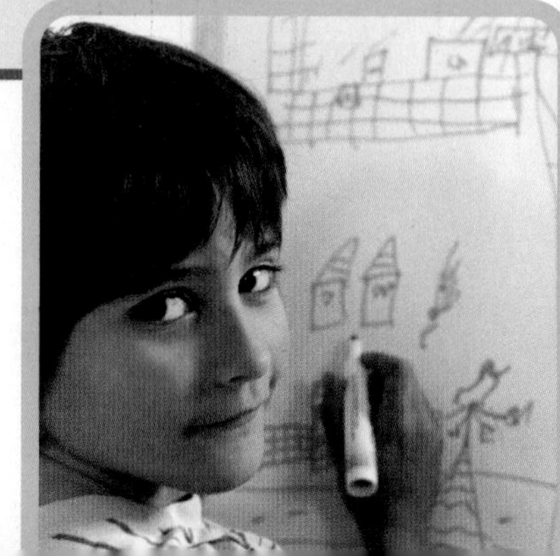

Trevor's values

Be responsible in your town

 82 **Listen and say the number.**

1
TRIANGELN

2

3

4

5

6

 **Look and say with a friend.**

We can recycle bottles.

Picture four.

Language: *We can wait / play / recycle here. / Don't cross.* | social responsibilities

Review Units 5, 6, 7 and 8

1 83 Listen and say the letter.

a

b

c

d

e

f

2 Read and answer.

Leo and Ivan are at the farm today. They're looking at the . Next to it there are three . They're eating 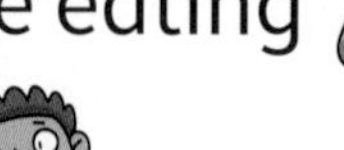. A  is . Ivan's very .

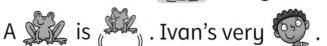

1 Where is Leo?

2 What are they looking at?

3 How many ducks are there?

4 What's the frog doing?

1 Play the game. Answer the question.

Where's the star?

It's in front of the hospital.

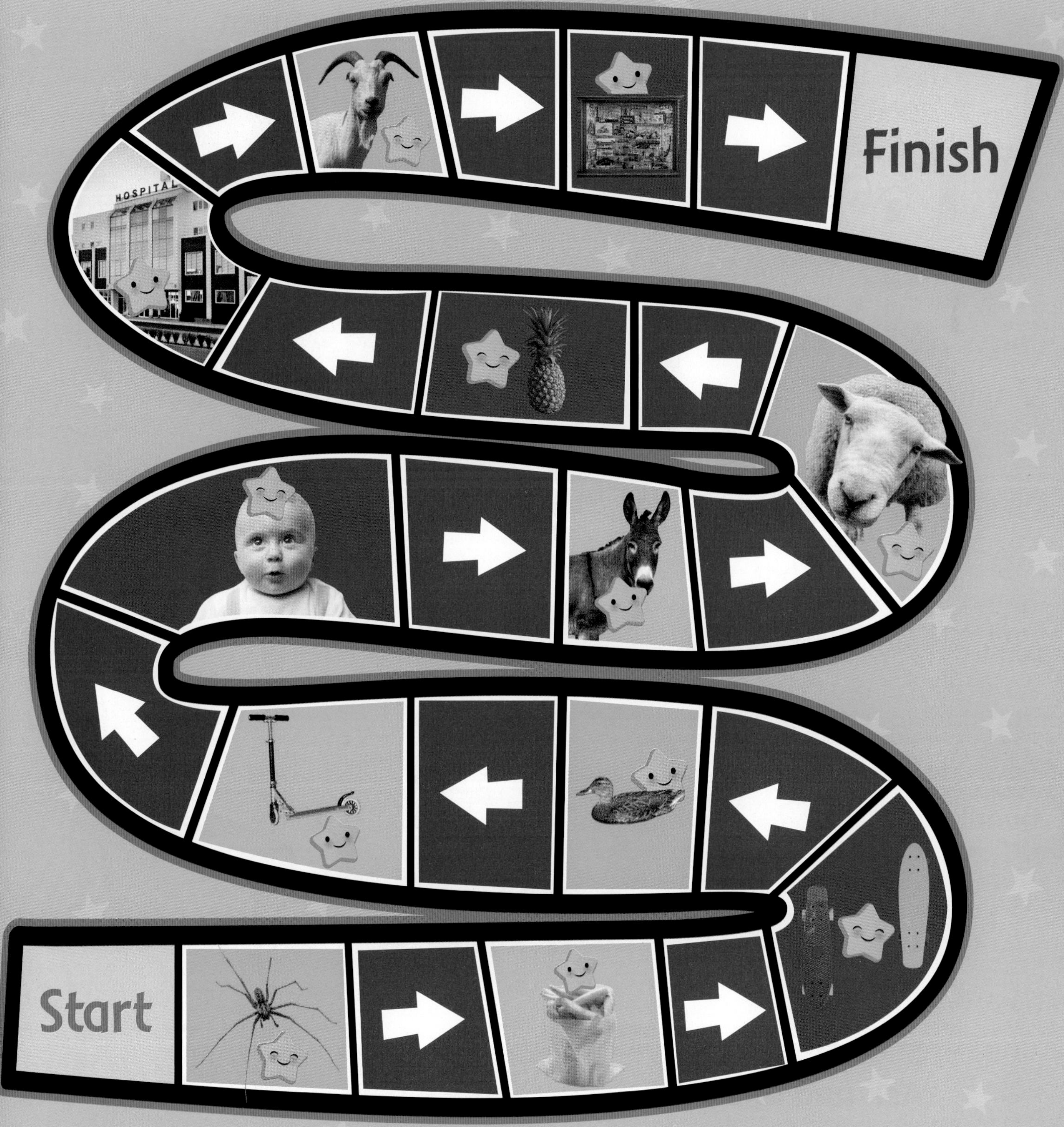

Start

Finish

HOSPITAL

9 Our clothes

1 84–85 Listen and answer. Listen and repeat.

sunglasses
shirt
jeans
hat
glasses
handbag
dress

2 Ask and answer.

What are these?
They're sunglasses.

9

1
86–87

Say the chant. Listen and correct.

There's a big box with toys.

No, there's a big box with clothes.

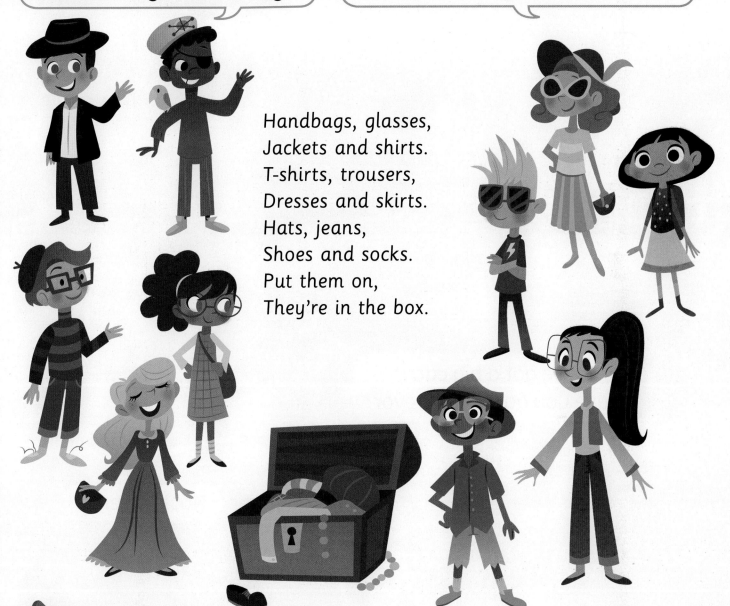

Handbags, glasses,
Jackets and shirts.
T-shirts, trousers,
Dresses and skirts.
Hats, jeans,
Shoes and socks.
Put them on,
They're in the box.

2 Read and say 'yes' or 'no'.

1 Two girls are wearing long pink dresses. No.
2 Three boys are wearing hats.
3 Two girls are wearing glasses.
4 Four boys are wearing sunglasses.
5 Two girls are wearing skirts.

1 88–89 Listen and point. Listen and repeat.
I've got a big car.
Have you got a car, Trevor?
No, I haven't.
2 Ask and answer.
Has Maskman got a blue car?
Yes, he has.

Language presentation 2: *have got* questions and answers *Have you got a big car? Yes, I have. / No, I haven't.*

1
90–91

9

Listen and sing. Do karaoke.

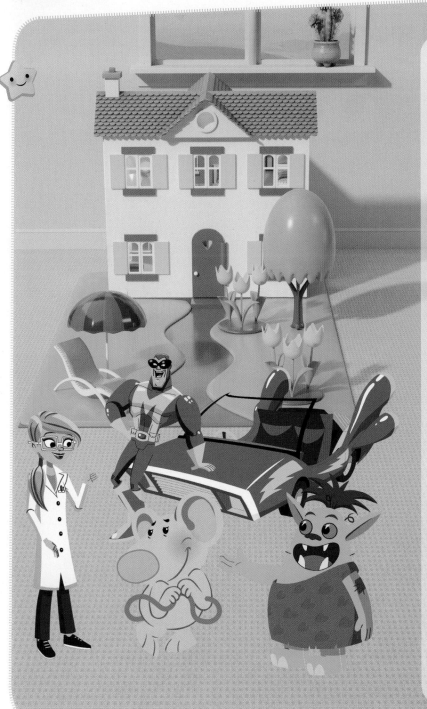

I've got a big garden,
I've got a big house.
I've got a good friend,
A small toy mouse.
I've got you, Monty.
I've got you.

Oh, Marie!

I've got a black mask,
And a big blue car.
I've got black glasses,
I'm the Maskman star,
And I've got you, Monty.
I've got you.

Oh, Maskman!

I haven't got
Superhero clothes.
I've got purple hair,
And a big green nose,
And I've got you, Monty.
I've got you.

Oh, Trevor!

I've got you, Monty.
I've got you.

2

Ask and answer.

Have you got a garden?

Yes, I have.

Monty's sounds and spelling

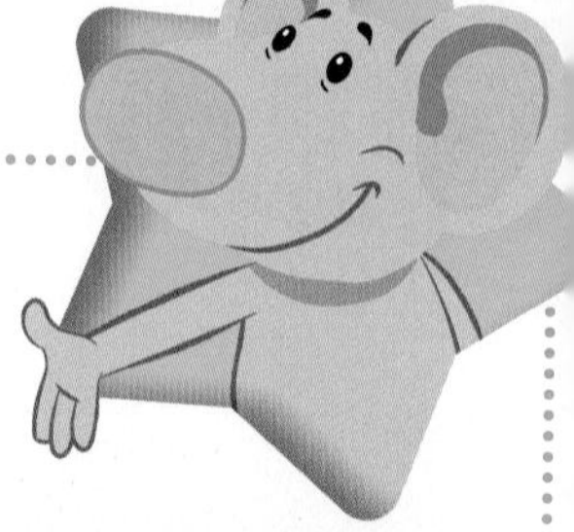

1 92 **Watch and say.**

A jellyfish in a jacket juggling jugs and juice!

2 Ask your friend.

Have you got sunglasses and
a yellow jacket in your picture?

No.

1
3
4
2
Write it with me!
__ ellyfish

1 93 Watch the video.

1
Monty! Are you wearing my long white jacket and my glasses?
Yes, I am. I'm Marie Mouse.

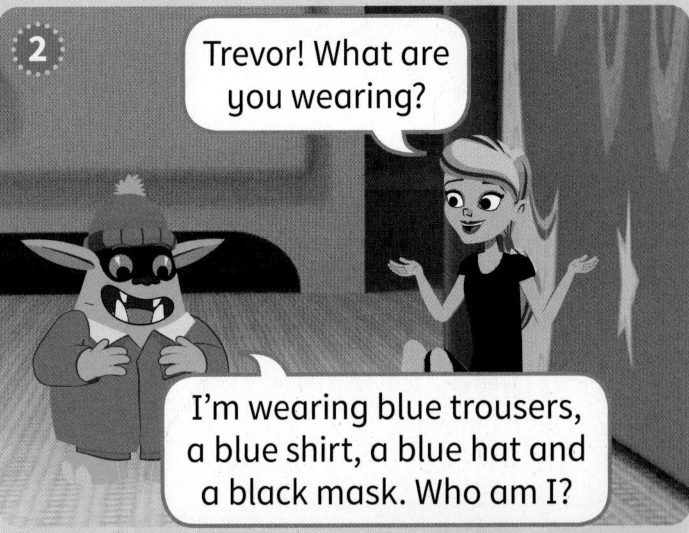
2
Trevor! What are you wearing?
I'm wearing blue trousers, a blue shirt, a blue hat and a black mask. Who am I?

3
I can swim and fly, but I can't sing or dance. I'm … Masktroll!

4
Look at Maskman!

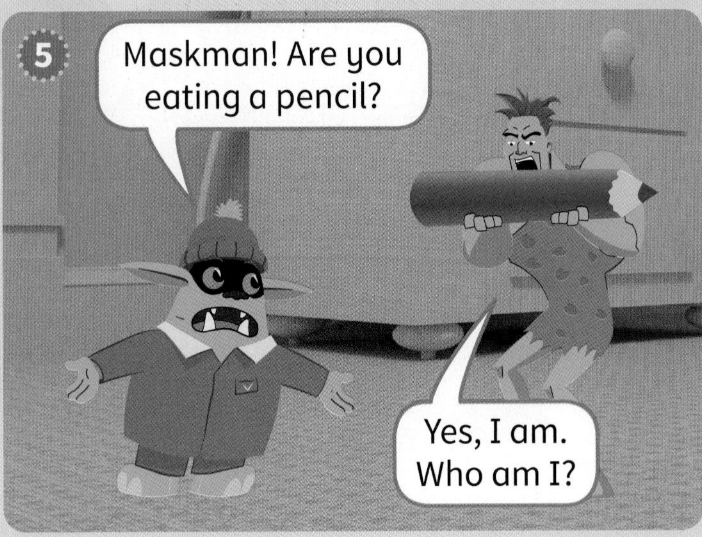
5
Maskman! Are you eating a pencil?
Yes, I am. Who am I?

6
You're … Trollman!
That's right! I can't swim and I can't spell.
No, you can't, Trollman, but you've got a lot of friends.

2 94 Listen and say the number.

10 Our hobbies

1 95–96 Listen and answer. Listen and repeat.

skateboarding

badminton

table tennis

painting

hockey

basketball

baseball

2 Play and say.

H-o-c-k-e-y!

Hockey!

1
97

Listen and match. Say the hobby.

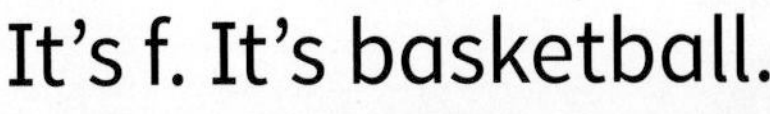

It's f. It's basketball.

2

Read and answer.

These children are playing football. This sport has got two names: football and soccer. In a football team, there are ten players who can run and kick the ball, and one player who can kick and catch the ball. This player is the goalkeeper. Can you see the goalkeeper in this picture? She's wearing an orange T-shirt, black shorts and yellow boots.

1 The children are playing
   - **a** badminton
   - **b** basketball
   - **c** football.

2 Eleven players can
   - **a** kick the ball
   - **b** catch the ball
   - **c** bounce the ball.

3 One player can
   - **a** run
   - **b** hit the ball
   - **c** catch the ball.

Listen and say the number.

Number three.

1 
Name: Grandpa Star
Likes: fishing and badminton
Dislikes: cleaning his shoes

2 
Name: Lenny
Likes: swimming and football
Dislikes: table tennis

3 
Name: Mr Star
Likes: the guitar and cooking
Dislikes: horses

4 
Name: Grandma Star
Likes: painting and driving
Dislikes: gardening

5 
Name: Meera
Likes: bikes and photos
Dislikes: TV

6 
Name: Alex
Likes: badminton and the piano
Dislikes: baseball

7 
Name: Simon
Likes: basketball and hockey
Dislikes: cleaning his room

8 
Name: Mrs Star
Likes: horses and reading
Dislikes: cooking

9 
Name: Suzy
Likes: singing and drawing
Dislikes: soccer

10 
Name: Stella
Likes: the piano and reading
Dislikes: doing sport

Say and play.

She likes horses and reading, but she doesn't like cooking.

Mrs Star.

Language presentation and practice 1: *I don't like / like / love singing. She likes / doesn't like cooking.*

10

1
99–100

Listen and sing. Do karaoke.

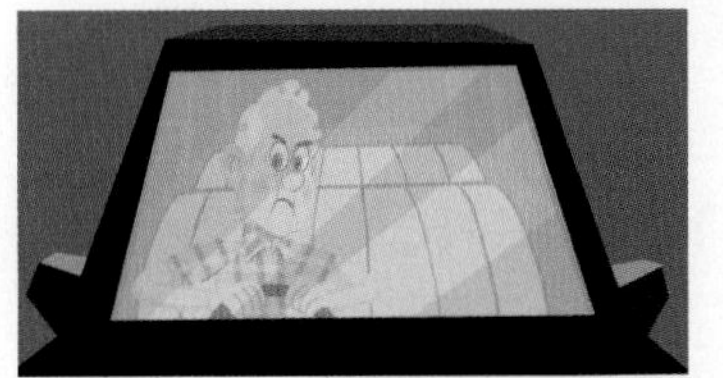

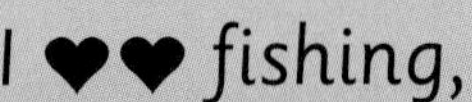

I ♥♥ fishing,
I ♥♥ flying kites,
I ♥ taking photos,
I ♥ riding bikes.
I ♥♥ fishing!
Bedum … bedoo.

I ♥♥ swimming,
Playing hockey too,
And I ♥♥ painting,
With the colour blue.
I ♥♥ swimming!
Bedum … bedoo.

I ~~♥~~ driving,
Or flying in a plane,
I ~~♥~~ cleaning shoes,
I ~~♥~~ running for a train!
Bedum … bedoo.

I ~~♥~~ cooking,
Or playing the guitar,
I ~~♥~~ badminton,
Or cleaning my dad's car.
I ~~♥~~ it!
Bedum … bedoo. Yeh!

2

Ask and answer.

Does Simon like painting?

Yes, he does.

Language presentation and practice 2: *Does Grandpa like (taking photos)? Yes, he does. / No, he doesn't.*

Monty's sounds and spelling

1 101 Watch and say.

The whale and the snail are playing baseball today.

2 Choose, draw and say.

The whale loves …

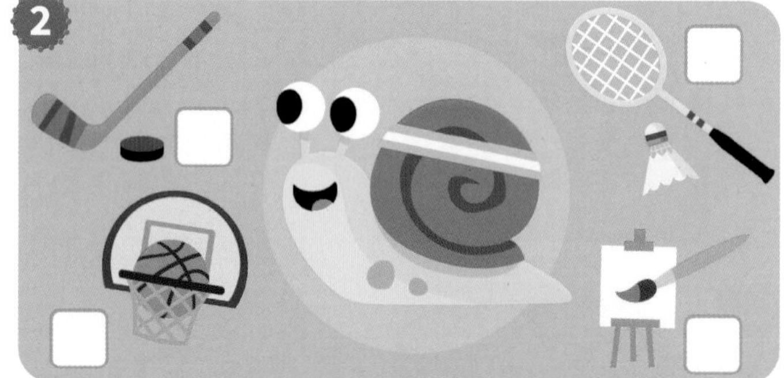

Write it with me!

The sn__ __l's pl__ __ing b__s__ball.

1 102 Watch the video.

1
What a great game of soccer! Yes! What a great goal!
18
15

2
Number 18 is kicking the ball. Now number 15 is hitting the ball with his head.
15

3
Ouch! My hands!
No, Maskman! You can't touch the ball with your hands!

4
Now number 15 is running with the ball.
15

5
Trevor! Are you eating the ball?
No, I'm not.
15

6
Come and play football with us, Marie!
Oh no, boys! I love reading about soccer, but I don't like playing it.
18
15

2 103 Listen and say 'yes' or 'no'.

Marie's sports

What sports can we do in summer and winter?

1 Watch and answer.

2 Read and match.

1 We can go mountain walking in summer.

2 I really like skiing when it snows.

3 Snowboarding is very popular in winter.

4 We like sailing in summer.

5 I love surfing in the big waves! I'm not scared!

6 I love snorkelling in the warm water.

a 

b 

c 

d 
4333

e 

f 
1

3 What summer and winter sports do you like doing?

Dogs like surfing, too! In the USA, there's a surfing competition for dogs every September.

Fact

Project

Do a hobbies survey.

Trevor's values

Follow the rules

104 **Listen and say the number.**

Look and say with a friend.

You can hit the ball with a bat.

Table tennis and baseball.

Language: *You can / can't (run with the ball).* | social responsibilities

11 My birthday

1 105–106 **Listen and answer. Listen and repeat.**

Happy Birthday Simon
sausages
salad
watermelon
cake
lemonade
oranges
pie

2 Play and say.

How many burgers are there?

There are two.

11

1
107

Listen and point. Say the chant.

Look at them
Five young men.
Look at him
He can swim.
Look at her
In her new skirt.
Look at you
And your nice clean shoe.
Look at us
On a big red bus.
Look at me
I'm under a tree.

2

Read and write.

Birthday party

It's my birthday __*party*__ this afternoon. Mum and Dad are doing things in the house and I'm helping them. Dad's in the kitchen. He's making a big **1** ________ for us. Mum's in the living room. She's putting a salad on the **2** ________ next to a big, green and red **3** ________ . There are a lot of burgers and **4** ________ . We've got **5** ________ to drink.

Example

party	sausages	table	hall
cake	watermelon	lemonade	bed

1 108–109 Listen and answer. Listen and repeat.

Happy Bi
Would you like some fries?
Juice
Lemonade
Yes, I'd love some.
Lemonade

Language presentation 2: *Would you like a burger or a sausage? I'd like a burger, please. Yes, I'd love one / some.*

11

1
110–111

Listen and sing. Do karaoke.

Pencils

Lemonade

I'd like a great big chocolate cake,
And I'd like one for me.
I'd like a nice long sausage,
And I'd like one for me.

I'd like a burger and some fries,
And I'd like some for me.
I'd like a drink of lemonade,
And I'd like some for me.

I'd like coloured pencils, ...
I'd like a box of coloured pencils,

Don't give any to me!

2

Ask and answer.

Would you like a burger?

Yes, please.

No, thank you.

Monty's sounds and spelling

1 112 **Watch and say.**

HAPPY BIRTHDAY

Happy birthday, purple bird.
Let's eat a burger at the circus!

2 **Say and play.** The girl's got some birthday cake. Picture 3!

1 2 3 4

Write it with me!

p___ple b___d

11

1

113 Watch the video.

1
It's Marie's birthday today.
Let's have a party for Marie! Let's make her a pencil cake.
Pencils
Lemon Cake Mix
No, Trevor. Marie would like a lemon cake.
3
Now let's make the cake.

2
Let's have burgers and fries to eat.
No, Maskman. It isn't your birthday.

4
Ssh. Marie's coming!
Now we can't make her a cake.

5
Happy birthday, Marie!

6
Thanks, boys! Would you like to come to the café with me?
Can I have some pencil cake, please?

2

Act out the story.

12 On holiday!

School

1 114–115 Listen and point. Listen and repeat.

mountain

sun

shell

sea

sand

beach

2 Ask and answer.

What can you see on the beach?

I can see sand.

Vocabulary presentation: the world around us

1
116–117

12

Listen and sing. Do karaoke.

I'm writing a new song,
I'm writing a new song.
At the beach, at the beach.

Suzy's getting lots of shells,
She's getting lots of shells.
At the beach, at the beach.

Simon's swimming in the sea,
Simon's swimming in the sea.
At the beach, at the beach.

Dad's walking on the sand,
Dad's walking on the sand.
At the beach, at the beach.

Mum's reading in the sun,
Mum's reading in the sun.
At the beach, at the beach …

2

Ask and answer.

What's Stella doing?

She's writing a song.

1 118 Listen and answer.
Do you want to go to a big city?
Where do you want to go on holiday?
I want to go to the mountains.
2 Play and say.
I want to go to the mountains.
I want to go to the mountains and I want to go to the beach.

Language presentation and practice 1: *Where do you want to go? I want to go to the mountains.*

1 Listen and point. Say the chant.

I want a
And you want some .
She wants some
And he wants some .

They want a
And we want a .
She wants a
And he wants a .

2 Listen and say the letter.

Which melon do you want?

I want the big green one.

That's m.

TOYS
Shoes
MARKET
OPEN
a
b
c
d
e
f
g
h
i
j
k
l
m
n
o
p

3 Read and circle.

Sue's on holiday with her **grandma / dad / cousin**. They're **in the mountains / at the beach / in the city**, and it's fun. This morning they're in a shoe shop. They're looking at some **boots / shoes / socks** for her holiday. Sue wants the **red / green / blue** ones. It's her favourite colour.

They go to a café for lunch. Sue wants **a pie and fries / meatballs and salad / sausages and beans** and she'd like ice cream, too. She can have chocolate, orange or banana ice cream. She wants **chocolate / orange / banana**. She loves ice cream!

1

Monty's sounds and spelling

1 121 Watch and say.

A purple cat with a kite in a tree
And a chicken painting a whale.
A hippo with a spider on its nose
And a jellyfish playing with a snail!

2 Say and play.

Is the girl drinking juice?

Yes!

1

2

3

Write it with me!

___icken, ___ale, hi___o and sn___l!

1 122 Watch the video.

1
Here we are in the mountains.
Look, I've got a postcard from Maskman.

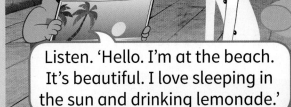

2
Listen. 'Hello. I'm at the beach. It's beautiful. I love sleeping in the sun and drinking lemonade.'

3
I want to go to 'Star Beach' and see Maskman.
OK, Trevor. We can go and find Maskman.

4
Hmm. I want my new dress, my new shoes … and my new sunhat and sunglasses.

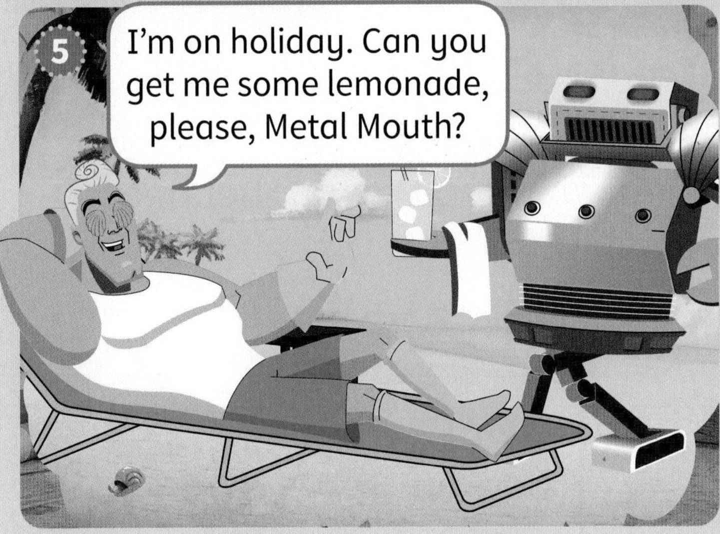
5
I'm on holiday. Can you get me some lemonade, please, Metal Mouth?

6
Maskman! Is this 'Star Beach'?
Hello. Er, yes, it is.
Ha ha ha.

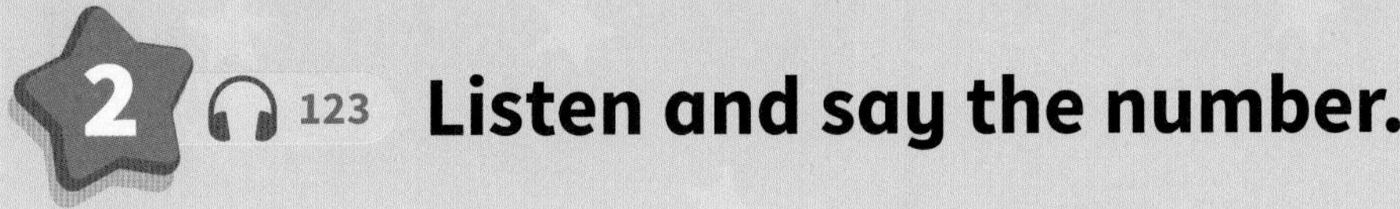

2 123 Listen and say the number.

Marie's geography

Where do you want to explore?

Watch and answer.

What do you need? Look and say.

In the caves I need …

In the sea …

In the mountains …

3 124 **Listen. Tick the boxes.**

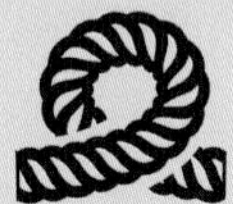

map ☐ rope ☐ torch ☐ air tank ☐ tent ☐

mask ☐ boots ☐ snorkel ☐ wetsuit ☐ helmet ☐

The Mammoth Cave in the USA is 650 kilometres long. You can choose from 15 different tours.

Fact

Project

Plan an adventure.

Trevor's values

Help on holiday

Read and match.

How can you help on your holiday?

a I'm Dev and I'm ten. I'm on holiday at an elephant park. It's cool! These elephants don't have a family. We give them a wash when they are dirty. Here, I'm giving a baby elephant a banana!

I love animals!

Dev

b I'm Jess. I'm a teacher and I'm on holiday in the mountains. The mountains are beautiful and green. I'm teaching these children outside!

It's fun. We are very happy!

Jess

c I'm Grace. I'm on holiday at the beach. The beach is dirty. There are a lot of plastic bottles and cups and the sea birds can't fly or swim.

I'm picking up rubbish with my friends and family.

Grace

125 Listen and say 'yes' or 'no'.

Grace is on holiday in the mountains.

No.

Review Units 9, 10, 11 and 12

1 🎧 126 Listen and correct.

The boy's wearing a green shirt.
No, he's wearing a red shirt.

2 Look and say with a friend.

In picture one the woman's reading, but in picture two she's writing.

1

2

1 Play the game.

Red square – Read and do
Blue square – What's this?
Green square – What's he/she doing?

Finish

You've got your sunhat. Go forward 2 squares.

You haven't got your sunhat. Go back 2 squares.

Your kite hasn't got a tail. Go back 1 square.

The sea's dirty. Go back 2 squares.

The sea's clean. Go forward 2 squares.

Start

Grammar reference

Who's he?	This is my brother, Simon. He's seven.
Who's she?	This is my sister, Suzy. She's four.

Who's he? = Who is he? he's = he is she's = she is

How many desks are there?	There are a lot of desks.
There's a ruler.	There isn't a ruler.
There are a lot of desks.	There aren't a lot of desks.
Is there a whiteboard? Are there ten desks?	Yes, there is. / No, there isn't. Yes, there are. / No, there aren't.

there's = there is there aren't = there are not

Whose is this camera?	It's Simon's.
Whose are these books?	They're Suzy's.

It's Simon's. = It's Simon's camera.
They're Suzy's. = They're Suzy's books.

Whose is that green T-shirt? Whose socks are those?	It's mine. They're yours.
Is that dress yours, Suzy? Are those socks yours, Simon?	Yes, it is. / No, it isn't. Yes, they are. / No, they aren't.
Which shoes are Simon's? Which shoes are Stella's?	The grey ones are his. The red ones are hers.

It's mine. = It's my T-shirt.

I'm He's / She's You're / They're / We're	singing.
I'm not	flying.
He's not / She's not / It's not (= He isn't / She isn't / It isn't)	
You're not / We're not / They're not (= You aren't / We aren't / They aren't)	
What are you doing, Suzy? What's Grandpa doing?	

Can I have some meatballs, please?	Here you are.

I love donkeys.	So do I. / I don't.

Where's the park?	It's	behind / in front of the shops.
Where are the flats?	They're	behind / in front of the shops.
Where's the school?	It's	between the café and the park.
Where are the shops?	They're	between the café and the park.

9

He's / She's They're	wearing blue shorts and white shoes. wearing sunglasses and big hats.	
Have you Has he/she	got a watch?	Yes, I have. / No, I haven't. Yes, he/she has. No, he/she hasn't.

haven't got = have not got hasn't got = has not got

10

I He/She	love / like / don't like loves / likes / doesn't like	swimming. playing table tennis.
Do you like reading?		Yes, I do. / No, I don't.
Does he/she like reading?		Yes, he/she does. No, he/she doesn't.

doesn't = does not

11

Look at me / you / him / her / it / us / them.	
Would you like a burger?	Yes, please. I'd love one.
Would you like some lemonade?	No, thank you. I'd like some juice.

12

Where do you want to go on holiday?	I want to go to the mountains.
Do you want to go to a big city?	I don't want to go to a big city.
Which shoes do you want?	I want the red ones.

Starters Listening

1 127 **Listen and write the question word. Choose and colour.**

What? How old? What number?

name questions = blue

number questions = orange

1 ______ is your family name?

2 ______ ______ is Lucy's sister?

3 ______ is the name of Tom's friend?

4 ______ ______ is Alex's house?

2 128 **Read the question. Look at the picture. Listen and write a name or a number. There are two examples.**

PARK

Examples

What is the name of Eva's cousin? Mark

How old is Eva's cousin? 11

Questions

1 What is Mark's family name? ______

2 How many paintings has Mark got in his house? ______

3 Which park does Mark like to go to? ______ Park

4 What number is Mark's house? ______

5 What is the name of the donkey? ______

Starters Listening

1 129 **Talk about the pictures. Then listen and look. Circle the correct picture.**

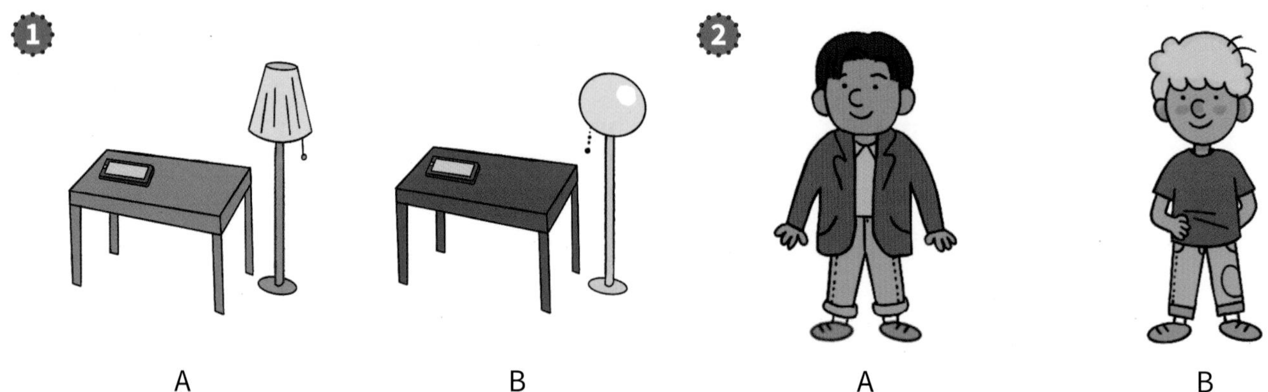

1
2
A
B
A
B

2 130 **Listen and tick (✓) the box. There is one example.**

Which is Bill's favourite toy?

A ☐ B ☐ C ☑

1 What sport is Anna doing this morning?

A ☐ B ☐ C ☐

2 Where is Mrs Watson's cat?

A ☐ B ☐ C ☐

3 What story is Grace reading?

A ☐ B ☐ C ☐

4 What is Tom eating?

A ☐ B ☐ C ☐

5 Which is Alex's house?

A ☐ B ☐ C ☐

Starters Reading and Writing

1 Look and read. Draw a line.

This is a T-shirt. These are shoes. This is a train.

1 

2 

3 

2 Look and read. Put a tick (✓) or a cross (✗) in the box. There are two examples.

Examples

This is an apple. ✓

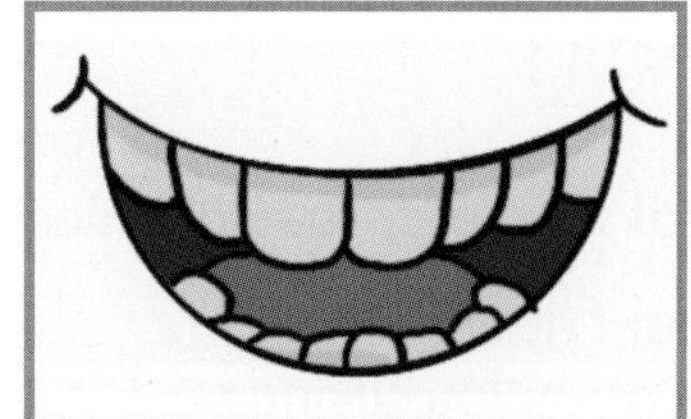

These are feet. 

Questions

1 

This is a skirt. ☐

2 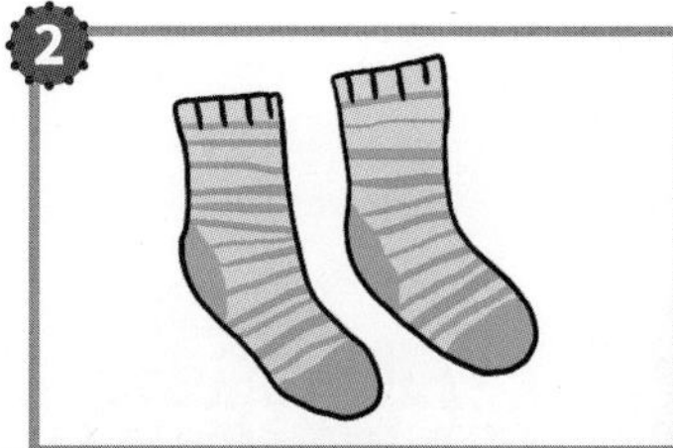

These are shoes. ☐

3 

This is a train. ☐

4 

This is a boat. 

5 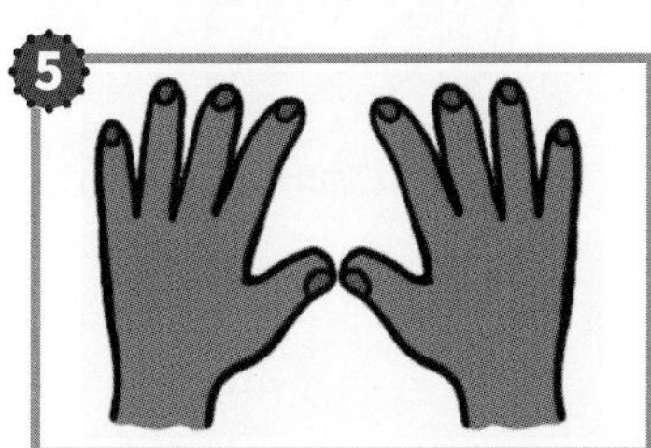

These are hands. ☐

Starters Reading and Writing

1 Read and circle the correct word.

1 Jellyfish live in the **park** / **sea**.
2 This monkey has got a long **tail** / **nose**.
3 **Lemons** / **Watermelons** are green and red.
4 A **kite** / **cat** is an animal.

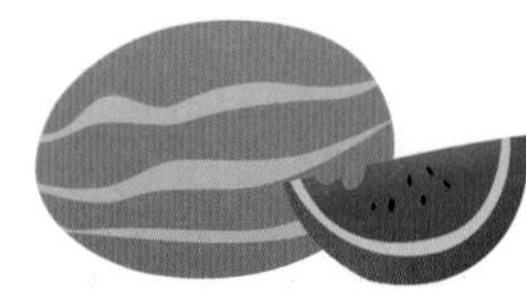

2 Read this. Choose a word from the box. Write the correct word next to numbers 1–5. There is one example.

Cats

Many people have a cat for a pet. They are nice, beautiful ___animals___ .

Cats live with you in your flat or (1) ______________ . They play with children's toys, for example small (2) ______________ . Cats enjoy sitting next to a window and watching (3) ______________ and lizards. In a garden, cats can run, jump on walls and climb (4) ______________ .

Cats love sleeping a lot too. They sleep in cupboards, under beds or on a (5) ______________ in front of the TV!

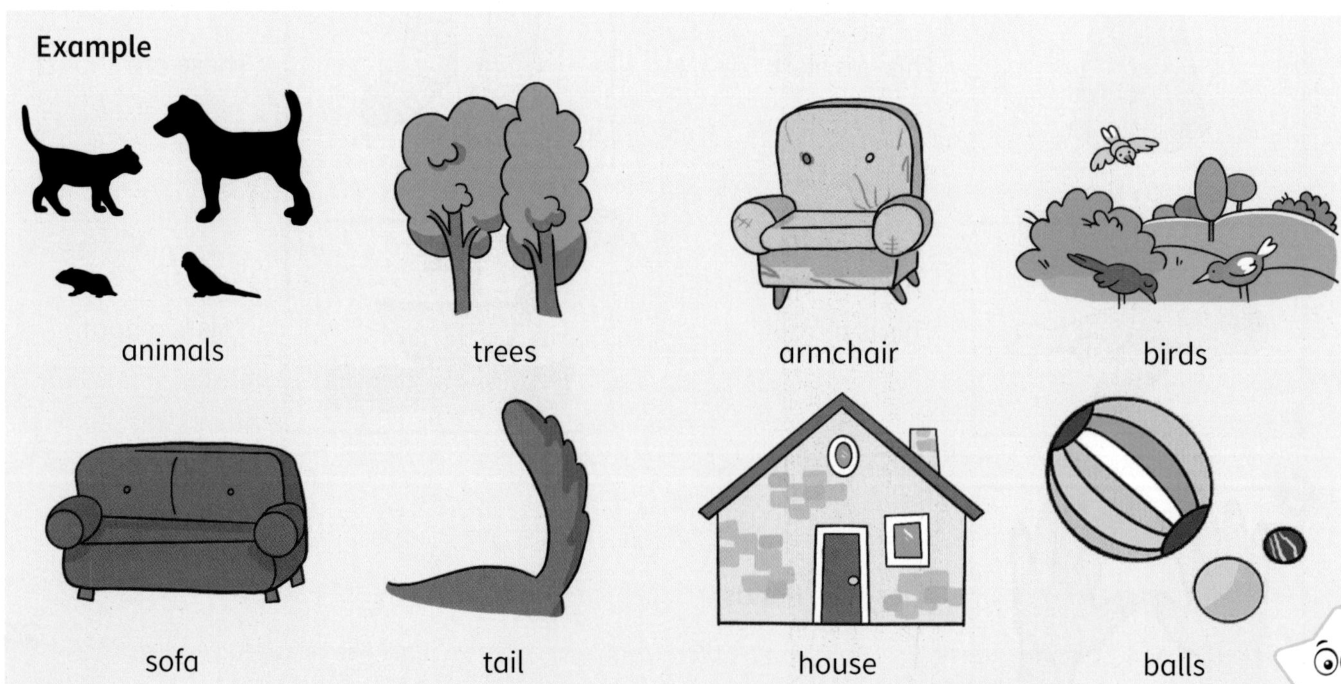

Example
animals
trees
armchair
birds
sofa
tail
house
balls

Starters Reading and Writing

1 Look and read. Write 'What', 'Where', 'Who' or 'How many'.

TOYS

______ are the children?	in a bedroom
______ is sitting on the bed?	the girl
______ is the girl holding?	a cat
______ ______ posters are there?	two

2 Look at the pictures and read the questions. Write one-word answers.

ZOO

Examples

Where are the people? in the park

What animal has the man got? a dog

Questions

1 What are the children doing? flying a ______

2 Who is pointing? the ______

3 Where is the dog? behind the ______

4 Which animal has got the kite? the ______

5 How many animals are there? ______

Starters Speaking

1 Look. Answer the questions with your classmate.

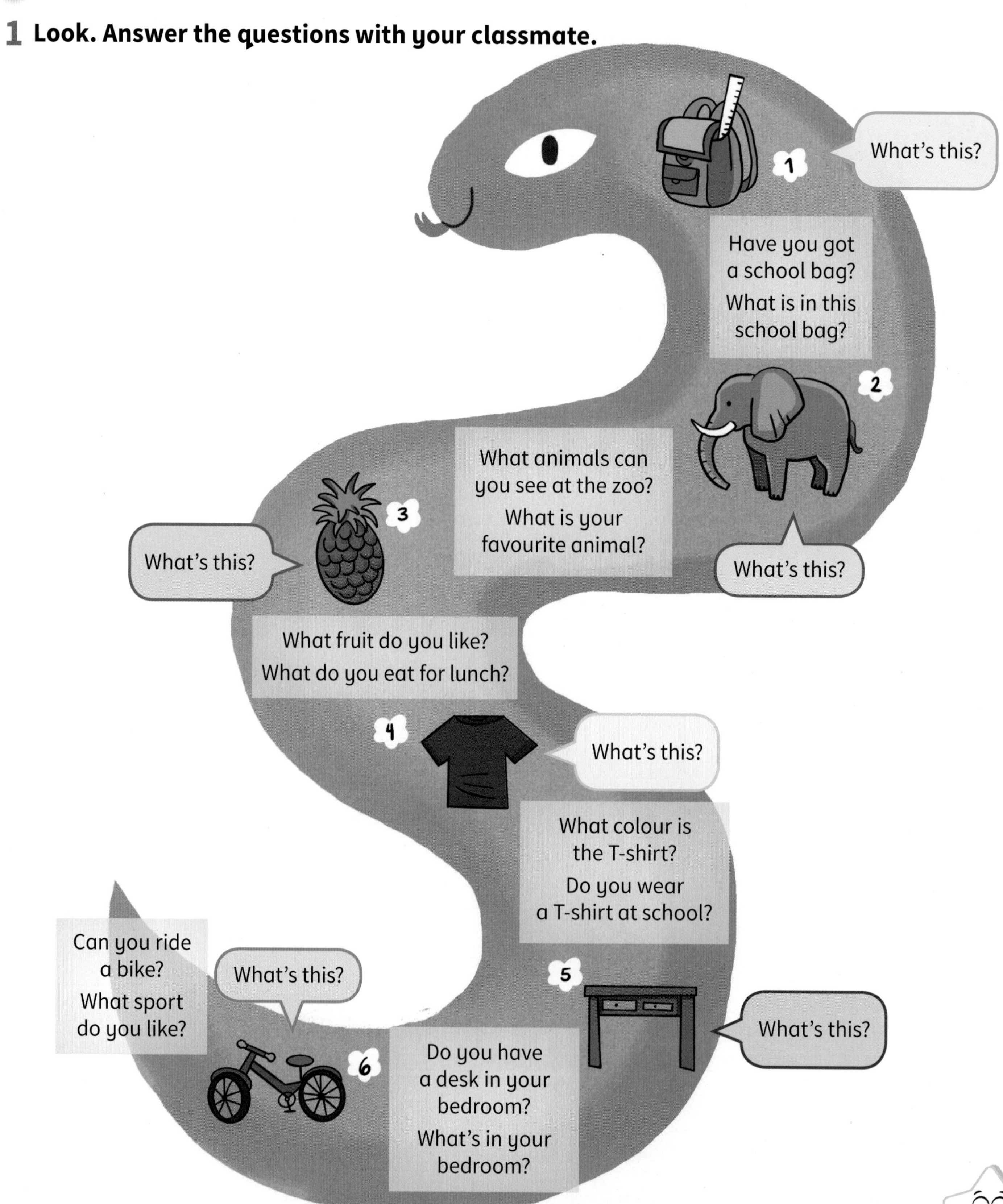

1
What's this?
Have you got a school bag?
What is in this school bag?
2
What's this?
What animals can you see at the zoo?
What is your favourite animal?
3
What's this?
What fruit do you like?
What do you eat for lunch?
4
What's this?
What colour is the T-shirt?
Do you wear a T-shirt at school?
5
What's this?
Do you have a desk in your bedroom?
What's in your bedroom?
6
What's this?
Can you ride a bike?
What sport do you like?

2 131 **Now look and listen. Answer the questions.**

Starters Speaking

1 132 **Look and listen. Write one word.**

1 Happy Birthday ______

2 ______

3 ______

4 ______

5 ______

6 ______

7 ______

8 ______

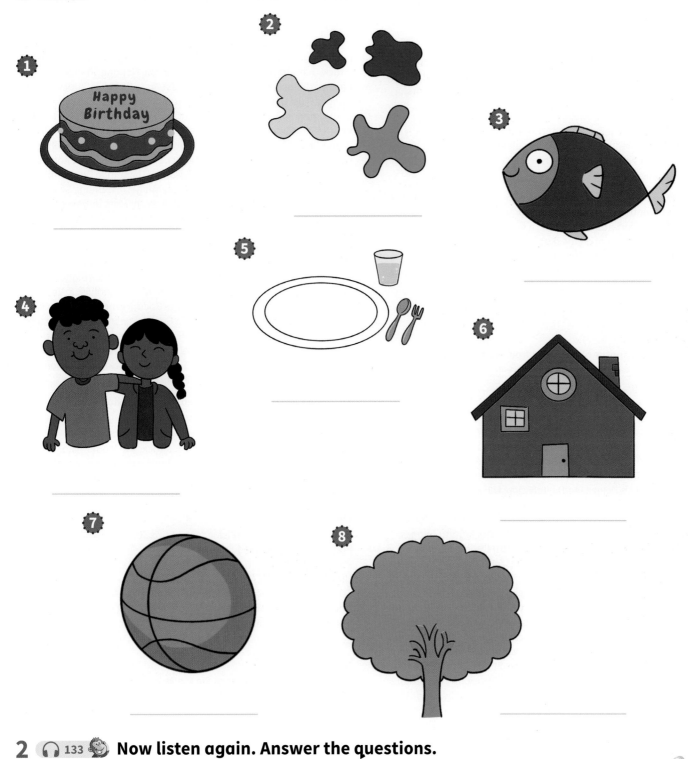

2 133 **Now listen again. Answer the questions.**

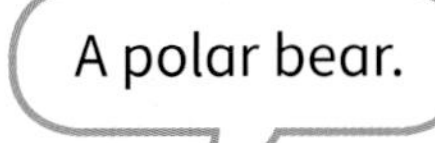
A polar bear.

A flat.

Thanks and Acknowledgements

Authors' thanks

Many thanks to everyone at Cambridge University Press for their dedication and hard work, and in particular to:

Liane Grainger and Lynn Townsend for supervising the whole project and guiding us calmly through the storms;

Alison Bewsher for her keen editorial eye, enthusiasm and great suggestions;

Amy Few and Liz Wilkie for their hard work, enthusiasm, and good ideas.

We would also like to thank all our pupils and colleagues, past, present and future, at Star English academy in Murcia, especially Jim Kelly for his friendship and support throughout the years.

Dedications

For my dearest sisters, Elaine and Teresa. We are Family. – CN
For my great friends in England, who always receive us so kindly, offering their warmth and friendship: Mike and Nicola, and Shaun and Lorraine. – MT

The authors and publishers acknowledge the following sources of copyright material and are grateful for the permissions granted. While every effort has been made, it has not always been possible to identify the sources of all the material used, or to trace all copyright holders. If any omissions are brought to our notice, we will be happy to include the appropriate acknowledgements on reprinting and in the next update to the digital edition, as applicable.

Key: U = Unit

Photography

The following photos are sourced from Getty Images.

U1: Anna Erastova/iStock/Getty Images Plus; **U2:** Science & Society Picture Library/SSPL; Ng Sok Lian/EyeEm; Zocha_K/E+; Thewet Nonthachai/EyeEm; Mosutatsu/E+; Gregor Hofbauer/Moment; Nehru Sulejmanovski/EyeEm; Theerasak Tammachuen/EyeEm; studiocasper/E+; Maria Kovalets/EyeEm; mikroman6/Moment; onebluelight/iStock/Getty Images Plus; Gelpi/iStock/Getty Images Plus; Drazen/E+; Ariel Skelley/Photodisc; monkeybusinessimages/iStock/Getty Images Plus; shironosov/iStock/Getty Images Plus; Indeed; Jose Luis Pelaez Inc/DigitalVision; **U3:** Anna Erastova/iStock/Getty Images Plus; **U4:** EKramar/iStock/Getty Images Plus; Sontaya Panyafu/EyeEm; BRULOVE/iStock/Getty Images Plus; vapadiii/iStock/Getty Images Plus; xmocb/iStock/Getty Images Plus; letty17/E+; hongquang09/iStock/Getty Images Plus; Jose Luis Pelaez Inc/DigitalVision; Rob Lewine; Ariel Skelley/Photodisc; prapassong/iStock/Getty Images Plus; Okea/iStock/Getty Images Plus; studiocasper/E+; ElementalImaging/E+; Bryan Mullennix; Jeffrey Coolidge/DigitalVision; MicroStockHub/iStock/Getty Images Plus; deepblue4you/iStock/Getty Images Plus; Aneduard/iStock/Getty Images Plus; Wladimir Bulgar/Science Photo Library; Image Source; akova/iStock/Getty Images Plus; MirageC/Moment; Hany Rizk/EyeEm; Alex Cao/Photodisc; in4mal/iStock/Getty Images Plus; D3Damon/iStock/Getty Images Plus; Snap Decision/Photographer's Choice RF; popovaphoto/iStock/Getty Images Plus; Westend61; vladru/iStock/Getty Images Plus; StockPlanets/E+; Bombaert Patrick/EyeEm; malerapaso/iStock/Getty Images Plus; Kim Sayer/OJO Images; Wa Nity Canthra/EyeEm; master-garry/iStock/Getty Images Plus; klyaksun/iStock/Getty Images Plus; Anna Erastova/iStock/Getty Images Plus; **U5:** Anna Erastova/iStock/Getty Images Plus; **U6:** Rusty Hill/Photolibrary; SDI Productions/E+; Piotr Krzeslak/iStock/Getty Images Plus; FotografiaBasica/iStock/Getty Images Plus; grau-art/iStock/Getty Images Plus; MAIKA 777/Moment; Kirill Strikha/EyeEm; Shannon M. Lutman/Moment; fcafotodigital/E+; Tom Werner/DigitalVision; Elizabeth Fernandez/Moment; Manuta/iStock/Getty Images Plus; Theerawat Kaiphanlert/Moment; gbh007/iStock/Getty Images Plus; The Picture Pantry/Alloy; Anna Erastova/iStock/Getty Images Plus; **U7:** Anna Erastova/iStock/Getty Images Plus; **U8:** Oleh_Slobodeniuk/E+; Matteo Colombo/DigitalVision; Raimund Koch/The Image Bank; Marco Bottigelli/Moment; Alexander Spatari/Moment; Kinzie Riehm/Image Source; Rebecca Nelson/The Image Bank; Daniel Llaó Calvet/EyeEm; kali9/E+; Todd Warnock/DigitalVision; Gareth Brown/The Image Bank; Nettiya Nithascharukul/EyeEm; Foodcollection; xavierarnau/E+; Pixel_Pig/E+; tbradford/iStock/Getty Images Plus; keiichihiki/E+; Honcha; Olivera Milijic/500px; andras_csontos/iStock/Getty Images Plus; Manuel Breva Colmeiro/Moment; Atanas Mahleliev/500px; Peter Cade/DigitalVision; tsingha25/iStock/Getty Images Plus; swetta/E+; Nancy Nehring/Photodisc; Anna Erastova/iStock/Getty Images Plus; **U9:** Anna Erastova/iStock/Getty Images Plus; **U10:** valda/iStock/Getty Images Plus; RapidEye/iStock/Getty Images Plus; TAPshooter/iStock/Getty Images Plus; valdecasas/iStock/Getty Images Plus; padnpen/iStock/Getty Images Plus; Oksana Struk/iStock/Getty Images Plus; damircudic/E+; A. Witte/C. Mahaney; David Samperio García/EyeEm; Holger Thalmann/Cultura; Rafael Ben-Ari/The Image Bank; Mikael Vaisanen/The Image Bank; mbbirdy/E+; Westend61; PacoRomero/E+; PeopleImages/E+; Image Source; Lorado/E+; Yoshiyoshi Hirokawa/DigitalVision; Marc Dufresne/E+; Anna Erastova/iStock/Getty Images Plus; **U11:** Anna Erastova/iStock/Getty Images Plus; **U12:** Amaia Arozena & Gotzon Iraola/Moment; ColorPlayer/iStock/Getty Images Plus; Christopher Hope-Fitch/Moment; Douglas Klug/Moment; Bonfanti Diego/Cultura; SolStock/E+; ViewStock; Cavan Images; Westend61; LueratSatichob/DigitalVision Vectors; VICTOR/DigitalVision Vectors; TongSur/DigitalVision Vectors; bubaone/DigitalVision Vectors; Levente Bodo/Moment; JGI/Tom Grill; Brett Stevens/Image Source; Antonio Garcia/EyeEm; LauriPatterson/E+; Rob Lewine; Suparat Malipoom/EyeEm; Yoshiyoshi Hirokawa/DigitalVision; hadynyah/E+; PeopleImages/E+; Genicio Zanetti Gz/EyeEm; Suriya Silsaksom/EyeEm; Thomas Barwick/DigitalVision; Roc Canals/Moment; Anna Erastova/iStock/Getty Images Plus.

The following photos are sourced from other libraries.

U4: romanklevets/Shutterstock; MasterPhoto/Shutterstock; Aron Brand/Shutterstock; Ingrid Balabanova/Shutterstock; Tanhauzer/Shutterstock; Mikael Damkier/Shutterstock; **U6:** Modernista Magazine/Shutterstock; New Africa/Shutterstock; Cagkan Sayin/Shutterstock **U8:** Phovoir/Shutterstock; LIGHTWORK/Shutterstock.

Commissioned photography by Copy cat.

Illustrations

Beatrice Costamagna, (Pickled ink); Chris Jones; Helen Naylor, (Plum Pudding); Kelly Kennedy, (Sylvie Poggio); Melanie Sharp, (Sylvie Poggio); Richard Hoit, (Beehive); Xian Xio, (Illustrationweb); Beth Hughes (The Bright Agency); Clara Soriano (The Bright Agency); Dan Crisp (The Bright Agency); Jake McDonald (The Bright Agency); Jen Naalchigar (The Bright Agency); Matthew Scott (The Bright Agency); Gaby Zermeno; Marek Jagucki; Pronk Media Inc.

Cover illustration by Pronk Media Inc.

Video

Video acknowledgements are in the Teacher Resources on Cambridge One.

Audio

Audio production by Creative Listening.

Design and typeset

Blooberry Design

Additional authors

Katy Kelly: Monty's Sounds and Spelling; Rebecca Legros: Marie's maths, art, geography, sports, and science; Montse Watkin: Exam folder.

Freelance editor: Pippa Mayfield